"*Daring to Live* gets your heart and faith muscles pumping as Sheri and her Dare Diva friends skydive, whitewater raft, hike Mount Kilimanjaro, and do all sorts of energetic, healing feats following the loss of her husband. Sheri's memoir is inspirational and deserves to be a bestseller."

**Jack Canfield**, coauthor of the Chicken Soup for the Soul series and *The Success Principles*

"In *Daring to Live*, Sheri Hunter illustrates the power of faith, overcoming fear, and living free. Her story will inspire you to live boldly and challenge you to explore the adventures of life. This powerful story of sisterhood as told through the eyes of Sheri, one of the four dynamic Dare Divas, inspired me so much! I'm excited for you to read this book. I know it will set you free the way it did for me!"

**DeVon Franklin**, Hollywood producer and *New York Times* bestselling author

"*Daring to Live* is a bold invitation into a life without limits. Through sharing her personal struggle with depression after a debilitating loss, Sheri reminds us that we're never too old, too young, or in too much pain to kick fear in the face. The power of sisterhood, revealed in her sharp wit and humorous storytelling, inspires us to live our days with a 'yes' in our hearts and a friend by our side. This book is a must-read for every person who wants to move from a mind full of fear to a life full of faith."

**Ashley Abercrombie**, author of *Rise of the Truth Teller*, speaker, and cohost of the *Why Tho?* podcast

"Sheri's story will enthrall you as she overcomes fear, loss, and grief. In her lowest moment she found life and adventure.

Her story is inspiring and empowering, and I pray that it instills courage in women everywhere. If you've ever felt held back by insecurities, this is the book for you."

**Jonathan Pokluda**, author of *Welcome to Adulting* and pastor of Harris Creek Baptist Church, Waco, Texas

"*Daring to Live* opens your eyes, heart, and soul to the importance of living life to the fullest and taking risks. Sheri's story will motivate you to live a life of strength, faith, and adventure while reminding you of the importance of friendship. Get ready to be inspired!"

**Karen Drew**, news anchor, WDIV-TV, Detroit

"We can all live a bold, daring life! In *Daring to Live*, Sheri Hunter shares that a truly bold life is lived in the small moments and by choosing what God has called us to do."

**Kelly Balarie**, speaker, blogger at *Purposeful Faith*, and author of *Fear Fighting* and *Battle Ready*

# daring to live

How the Power of Sisterhood
and Taking Risks Can
JUMP-START YOUR JOY

## SHERI HUNTER

**BakerBooks**
*a division of Baker Publishing Group*
Grand Rapids, Michigan

© 2020 by Sheri Hunter

Published by Baker Books
a division of Baker Publishing Group
PO Box 6287, Grand Rapids, MI 49516-6287
www.bakerbooks.com

Printed in the United States of America

Library of Congress Cataloging-in-Publication Data
Names: Hunter, Sheri, 1967- author.
Title: Daring to live : how the power of sisterhood and taking risks can jump-start your joy / Sheri Hunter.
Description: Grand Rapids : Baker Books, a division of Baker Publishing Group, 2020.
Identifiers: LCCN 2019027435 | ISBN 9780801094095 (cloth)
Subjects: LCSH: Hunter, Sheri, 1967- | Widows—Biography. | Christian women—Biography.
Classification: LCC BV4908 .H86 2020 | DDC 277.3/083092 [B]—dc23
LC record available at https://lccn.loc.gov/2019027435

Some names and details have been changed to protect the privacy of the individuals involved.

Emojis in chapter 7 are taken from OpenMoji.org.

20  21  22  23  24  25  26        7  6  5  4  3  2  1

In keeping with biblical principles of creation stewardship, Baker Publishing Group advocates the responsible use of our natural resources. As a member of the Green Press Initiative, our company uses recycled paper when possible. The text paper of this book is composed in part of post-consumer waste.

For my children,
David and Danielle

# contents

# introduction

I set out for a whitewater-rafting adventure on West Virginia's Gauley River with three of my closest girlfriends. Brenda, Angenette, Mia, and I had met two years earlier through the outreach ministry at our church. We quickly bonded over our shared life experiences, our Christian faith, and the fact that we—four middle-aged, African American women living in Detroit—wanted a little more adventure in our lives.

One Sunday afternoon, Mia—always the woman of action—walked into a ministry meeting with information on whitewater rafting. Fed up with all our talk of having an adventurous girls' weekend, she put a plan in motion.

"C'mon, Sheri! It'll be fun!" Mia said as I skeptically paged through the pamphlet she'd practically poked my eye out with minutes earlier.

"I don't know," I said slowly. "It seems kind of dangerous, seeing that none of us can, you know, *swim*."

"But that's why it will be an adventure!" Mia winked. "What's an adventure without a little danger?"

"Yessss, let's go," Ang said. "So great I found like-minded women who like adventure. I've whitewater rafted before. It's so fun."

Mia and Ang were so excited, but it was unusual for me to consider doing something like this. Still, I was at a point in my life where I wanted to live outside myself a bit.

"Okay, I guess so." I gave a half smile. "I'm down!"

Brenda was the last to agree. Like me, she didn't know what we were getting into, but she was willing to give it a go.

The morning we left, I hugged my kids real tight and kissed my husband, Mannard, goodbye as I headed out the door.

Mannard stopped me, not letting go of my hand as I tried to walk to the car. He gave me a pointed look. "Remember to have *fun*," he said, arching his eyebrows. "Don't hold yourself back on this trip because of the what-ifs."

I gave him a thin-lipped smile. If there was anything I'd learned over seventeen years of marriage to this man, it was that he always knew what I was feeling, whether I expressed it or not. "Okay, I won't," I said, avoiding his eyes and darting out the door.

The next day, as I stood in front of the massive, churning Gauley River, Mannard's words ran through my mind. I felt my heart slide into the pit of my stomach. I was *terrified*. I could not swim, so how was I supposed to deal with a hostile river that seemed primed to toss any one of us overboard? Had I embarked on the equivalent of a suicide mission?

Angenette was the only one who had whitewater rafted before, when she lived in California. She was a true diva, bringing all her adventurous spirit, as she had skydived and traveled to South Africa—things that made my head spin. Mia and Ang were inspiring me.

We were assigned to a raft with a sturdy-looking forty-something and his teenage son. As Katy, our guide for the day, went over the safety precautions in detail, I fidgeted with my life jacket, trying to ascertain whether it was sufficiently buoyant to hold my weight in the very likely chance I got thrown into the drink.

Our adventure began smoothly enough. I was lulled into a stupor, looking at the beautiful wooded areas surrounding the river. The frightening rapids I'd seen in the pamphlet must have been for the experienced paddlers only, I reasoned. Boy, was I wrong.

Within minutes, so much water had crashed over my head and spilled down my throat, I thought I'd be sick. My water shoes clung to the floor of the blue urethane raft as I gripped the rope inside it. I dug deep, ready for the next wave to hit. I'd situated myself at the back of the raft, since Katy had designated the very front as the "wallop zone"—the area where you had better take one big gulp of air because you'll likely hover at the top of the swirling West Virginia river a good many seconds before plunging over the rapid.

As another rapid approached, I held on to the rope. I clenched my teeth and tasted a bit of blood as I accidently bit my cheek. Brenda and Ang screamed as a giant wave washed over them, trying to slink away from the wave without going overboard. There was nowhere to go to get away from the onslaught of freezing water; we simply had to endure it.

The next rapid quickly approached. It seemed smaller than the previous one, but I was ready. Katy sat high on the backside of the raft, working her paddle to navigate the craft headfirst into the circling undercurrent. We slammed hard into another raft and then bounced up against a giant rock. I flew out of my seat, nearly dropping my oar into the river. Out of the corner of my eye, I saw the flash of an object dropping like a rock into the rapids.

"Katy is in the water!" someone shouted. We all paddled as hard as we could toward her, even though the strong currents were moving our raft away from her and down the river. Her eyes widened with either fear or mortification that the raft was floating away with her paying customers on board.

Luckily, another guided reft had seen what happened and steered over to assist us with our rescue. As the leader of the other raft shouted directions at us, I was surprised to see Katy swimming with all her might toward us—and making headway, no less! Our frantic paddling and Katy's efforts got us within range of each other, and she was able to grab on to Angenette's oar as Brenda and I helped to haul her back on board.

"You guys okay?" Katy said, looking up at us through wet eyelashes.

"Are *we* okay? No, are *you* okay?" Ang asked.

We all laughed, relieved our commander was back at the helm.

At the end of our day, Katy led us to a rocky cliff that people were climbing. Four rafts were floating along the shore, and at the top of the cliff a line of about fifteen people waited to jump into the river.

"Nope, not doing that," Ang said matter-of-factly, and positioned herself to relax inside the raft, tucking her legs along the seat cushions.

We watched in awe as people jumped from the cliff and swam back to their rafts. Those who remained on board helped hoist them back into the raft. For someone who had never even jumped into a swimming pool, the idea of hurtling forty feet into the water gave me more than a moment of pause.

Mia looked at us with a mischievous smile and informed us she was jumping. "Y'all coming?" she asked.

I looked at the line. There wasn't one African American face in the bunch, nothing black or brown except for the bark on the elms whispering, "Sheri, don't do it. Stay in the raft with the wise Angenette."

But something inside me told me to rebel. I remembered Mannard's words: *Don't hold yourself back on this trip because of the what-ifs.*

Soon I was following Mia up the side of the cliff, with Brenda reluctantly following behind. On the way up, I nearly fell face-first over a particularly small rock. I had no idea how I was going to make it to the top without fracturing my ankle, let alone jump when I got there!

I heard myself say, "I can't, Mia. I want to go back."

"Don't turn back now," said a tall, lean guy walking near us. "It's more treacherous going down than continuing up."

I looked over my shoulder. He was right. I would definitely crash-land trying to get back down. There was no option but to continue up the trail.

Standing at the top, I felt like I had conquered Mount Everest. I would have been fine putting that in my journal as the day's accomplishment, but with the rickety rock pile behind me, there was only one way down—I had to jump. The line was getting shorter and shorter.

Mia shook all her limbs as if shaking the fear out of her body. She stepped back a few feet, then jogged toward the cliff and jumped.

Brenda and I looked at each other in surprise. "Man, she did it!" Brenda said.

"Yep." I peeked over the edge in time to witness the voluminous splash. Katy and Angenette paddled toward Mia, using the oars to hoist her into the raft.

"Okay, Bren, it's on you." I gave her a thumbs-up.

Brenda responded with a killer side eye. "I thought *you* were next."

The two of us hemmed and hawed while the line grew steadily longer behind us. I realized that she was as frightened as I was. I clasped her hand. "Let's do it together."

"One," Brenda said. We looked eye to eye.

"Two," I said as we scooted closer to the cliff's edge.

"Three," we said in unison, and leapt as if our lives depended on it.

I felt the pull of gravity as my stomach lurched to my throat. Our hands somehow dislodged, and Brenda accelerated to move ahead of me. I didn't look down and kept my eyes closed. I held my breath and heard a splash. It wasn't me.

When was I going to hit the water? I was moving alone in time, and though I knew that the inevitable submersion was coming, I was uncertain how the impact would feel.

I hit the water like a torpedo, water filling my nose and mouth. Somehow, with all that $H_2O$ around me, I felt a big smile form on my face. I surfaced and heard Brenda's laughter as she was hoisted into the raft. Then it was my turn. They pulled me in, and I crashed onto the floor of the vessel.

Breathless, I grinned at my friends. "I'd do it again!"

They just laughed. The truth was that we all wanted to be bounced here and there. A gentle, tranquil day on a lazy river would have been an epic fail. No one wanted that—not even me.

I have since learned that's true of my life as well. While I say I desire serenity, after a while it becomes mundane and tiresome. There's a deep dissatisfaction that festers inside me when things sit still, making me crave a more challenging world—a world that requires more of me and forces me to live up to my full potential.

What will challenge you?

. . .

That adventure was the first of many I would go on with my sister-friends. We would eventually call ourselves the Dare Divas, a name that reflected our sassy attitudes and penchant for extreme activities. Together we learned to ski, drive motorcycles, and parachute out of airplanes. The four of us had grown up in inner-city Detroit, so to say that these feats were things we'd never dreamed of doing is a vast understatement—and yet it seemed that together we could accomplish anything.

When I think back to that whitewater trip with my friends, I can see how the Lord helped me develop friendships and forge ahead through challenges, which prepared me for the devastating summer of 2012, when the unthinkable happened. On a rainy August morning in 2012, I awoke around four o'clock to what sounded like a broken water pump in the basement. I reached over to wake up Mannard so he could deal with the pump. Those bumps in the night were his job.

When he didn't respond, I looked over and realized *he* was the source of the offending sound. His hands were balled into fists; his eyes bulged. His once beautiful cocoa-brown face was ashen. He was arched eerily heavenward, struggling for air, unable to speak.

"Baby! Mannard!" I shouted.

He didn't respond.

I slid onto the hardwood floor, nearly tripping over my nightgown to dial 911.

I rushed to my son's room to wake him up. He was solidly snoring, and I grabbed him and dragged him across the floor.

"What's going on, Mom?"

"Help me! It's Dad!"

Back in my bedroom, I heard my seventeen-year-old man-child cry out like he was five years old when he saw his dad. We both did some version of CPR with my hands on Mannard's chest, my son's hand on his dad's forehead, but seconds later my husband stopped the awkward jerking as his spirit obeyed what was to be.

My son and I both let go as we watched my husband, his dad, breathe out—slowly, rhythmically, like he was expelling the last remnants of air from his lungs. As the doorbell rang downstairs, my son and I watched as one solitary tear slid from Mannard's face to the pillow. He was just fifty.

●  ●  ●

When I lost Mannard, I faced deep sorrow and shock, of course. But I distinctly remember that one feeling overshadowed all the others: supreme abandonment. This feeling was so permeating, it led me to question my long-held relationship with Jesus and my place in life itself.

During those first few weeks, the pain inside ate away at me. I turned to some destructive habits. Fortunately, the Dare Divas were there to pick me up, turn me toward God, and use our adventures together to help me heal. Our dares took on a therapeutic role. As I reflected on each challenge, I saw that God was using the dares to teach me a series of life lessons for my new life without Mannard.

My friendship with these women not only strengthened my resolve and joy for life, it renewed my personal relationship with God. I began seeking the Lord in ways I had never before dared to. Jesus was calling me to embrace his way of living, to walk in faith every moment of the day, and to develop greater discipline so I could have a more satisfying, fulfilling life.

Through the dares, I learned to step outside my comfort zone to follow where God led. Much like with jumping off that cliff, there was no going back. God was calling me to be a better mother to my children, a better friend to the Divas, a better custodian of the finances Mannard had lovingly stewarded during his life, and a beacon of hope to others who were dealing with profound loss.

We can all live a bold, daring life. This doesn't mean we have to face rushing rapids or jump off a cliff. A truly bold life is lived in the small moments, by choosing what God has called us to do. It's not letting the what-ifs hold us back. It's loving extravagantly, helping those in need, and being a good friend through the peaks and valleys of life. God calls us to journey outside of our comfort zones and propels us to live miraculous lives and try new things.

As I navigated my way through my sorrow and depression following Mannard's death, it wasn't a straight path to healing. There were times I'd take two steps toward feeling confident and strong, then jump five steps back. My story does not flow in a neat timeline. At times when the dare commenced and was completed, the lesson was potent, and that very day I felt myself growing in strength. Other dares took months, years even, for me to absorb the lesson and see the power of God's love and how he carried me through.

These dares, though not chronological, demonstrate how healing has been for me: a slow, steady realization of my own resilience, God's grace, and the power of friendship. I was on a Dare Diva adventure. Do you dare to join me?

# 1

# dare to care

when you need friends and God sends them

**JULY 2007**

The Dare Divas began at Christian Tabernacle Church (CTab), and the more we served together, the more my camaraderie with Brenda, Angenette, and Mia grew. The Contact Outreach and Development Ministry (CODM)—which included sharing the grace of salvation, discussing the significance of baptism, acquainting new members with the Christian walk, and having a decent amount of fun—was sometimes formidable, but it was a joy to see people grow in their walk with the Lord.

Each year, CTab held an all-church picnic. One of the events, the Armor Bearer Competition, was a stiff contest between ministries. The challenge contained a series of inflatable obstacles like on the TV show *American Ninja Warrior*.

None of us were highly trained athletes able to scale thirty-foot props designed to torpedo us into oblivion. But at the annual event you'd see Christians who were humble on Sundays go rogue in an effort to crush the competition.

"Listen, guys," Mia said, "we have to put on our superhero capes and run like we are Olympic gold medalists. I'm not playing with anybody. We have to win this." Mia was CODM's coach, and she took her job so seriously she came just short of brandishing a whip. "I don't want to hear anything about any knee or joint pain, because I've seen you all run for those donuts and hot coffee before church."

We laughed. Mia was not alone in her passion. The whole church got a bit frenzied over this yearly competition.

"Look," Ang said, "I'm not gonna break my neck hurling myself down that giant slide. Not gonna happen."

Lola, our friend who served in the pastoral care ministry, sauntered by and overheard Angenette. "Just give up, ladies and gents," she said. "We have police officers and professional security members in our ministry. You all are too soft."

"I got this," Angenette said, ready to confront Lola. We all knew that Ang, the attorney/counselor, was about to preach. Among the Dare Divas, she was the straight shooter and also the resident comic. She could make us fall on the floor in tears with laughter.

"Come on, now," Brenda said, smiling nervously. "Remember we are children of God. And while this is a competition, no need to act ungodly."

Ang looked at Brenda. "Sis, we know all that." Then she turned to Lola and said, "But they still about to get whipped. Because, Lola, my sis, we don't need police or security strength. We are gonna win with the Holy Spirit power of God!"

"Amen," I said, laughing.

"Down with them all and hallelujah," Mia said, wrapping her arm around my shoulders in solidarity.

We had so much fun that day. Old and young alike tumbled over the expansive church lawn like teenagers. With the exception of a few mild abrasions and a bruise or two, there were no major injuries. The CODM team didn't win; pastoral care did—easily. But that didn't stop us from looking forward to a rematch the following year.

Soon the closeness of serving and playing side by side bled over into the personal lives of each of the Dare Divas. We confided in one another and reached out for counsel and prayer on the big and small things going on in our lives. We would talk in person or text when we needed immediate counsel and support.

If one of us was sick, the others would bring groceries or a meal. Sometimes we'd just sit with the recovering Diva, binge-watching a favorite TV show or talking about life, jobs, marriage, and children. God granted us a special camaraderie that brought joy and sweetness into all of our lives.

We all have been there for each other, and we've opened our hearts to love each other. We know it was the Lord who facilitated that blessed day when we met in 2005. Back then, Mannard and I were raising a young family, and even though we were truly content, I felt a restlessness. I wanted to develop friendships but didn't know where to turn.

Maybe you have experienced a time where you longed for deep, abiding friendship but were not certain how to go about attaining it. It can be difficult for all of us to find like-minded people.

This was the place I found myself when I suddenly had an awakening to my need for friendship beyond my husband. Mannard and I had been married six years, and the kids were two and three. Though I loved my life, I felt isolated. At the time, Mannard seemed A-OK with his three friends—Alpha Phi Alpha frat brothers from the University of Pennsylvania who were solidly planted miles away from Detroit in Philadelphia. The four were perfectly content with their quarterly twenty-minute telephone chats about career, football, and family. But I felt like something was missing.

One day I broached the subject with Mannard. Our son, David, had just been kicked out of preschool for biting a girl in his class. "Don't you just want to talk to someone about what you're dealing with?" I asked.

"Nah, that's why I have you." Mannard was keeping an eye on the kids while I packed snacks for their upcoming overnight stay with my in-laws.

"That's sweet, babe," I said. "Maybe I'm just different. I need more human connection. More girl talk." I wiped the stove and stuffed baggies of Cheerios and bite-size grapes into a sack.

"We *are* different," he said. "I can talk to my friends on occasion, and that's enough for me. But you should get your girl talk. Find some friends."

"I'm your friend, Mommy," David said sweetly.

I stooped down and kissed my little biter on the forehead. "I know, pumpkin."

22

Mannard picked up Danielle from her high chair and placed her on his hip. "Dang, little girl, you feel soggy." He bumped his nose with hers and she giggled.

"Look, I'm good," he said to me. He kissed me on the cheek as he headed for the stairs and Danielle's changing table. "I don't really need more friends. But I want you to be good too."

Our daughter patted the back of her daddy's neck with her chubby hand and leaned her face into his broad shoulder. The two of them ascended the stairs, completely satisfied.

So why wasn't I?

Shortly after that conversation I met the three women who would have a profound impact on my life and become lifelong friends and fellow adventurers. At the time, Brenda and her husband, Idowu (I.D.), led the Contact Outreach and Development Ministry at our church.

Mannard and I had been talking about how to spend more time together, since his job as an IT consultant had him crisscrossing the US. We thought volunteering together at church was the perfect opportunity. As it turns out, a few weeks later our pastor asked Mannard and me to serve in the CODM.

At the informational meeting, Brenda welcomed six newcomers to the outreach ministry. "Pastor and Sister Morman said they picked individuals for this team who have loving and patient hearts," Brenda said, smiling warmly. "And as I look around, I feel it. I know we're going to do a mighty thing through Christ."

I smiled, catching her enthusiasm.

"Plus you're the only ones willing to volunteer for forty hours per week," I.D. chimed in with a chuckle.

"Don't scare them off, I.D.," Brenda said, swatting her husband. "It's not *quite* forty hours."

Mannard arched an eyebrow in my direction, giving me his classic "what have you gotten us into now?" look. Brenda passed out some large binders with colored tabs, outlining ministry policies and procedures. She looked sharp in her pin-striped navy suit, having just come from her job as a state public health administrator.

"Put me to work," said Mia, a woman with a tousled pixie cut. "Just so you know, I'm good at PowerPoint, Excel, pivot tables—any document, any data, I can put into a chart. I'm here to serve in any way." Mia's energy was contagious. I would learn that she was also a vice president and auditor for a bank.

"Wow, yes and yes!" Brenda said. "Thanks for sharing. We will try to put those skills to use."

"This is some binder," Angenette said, holding the massive thing in her arms like a bag of concrete. She may have been a lawyer for a major automobile manufacturer, but I could already tell she had a wicked sense of humor.

"I was thinking the same thing," I said, shooting a smile her direction. "All the information we'd ever need to know and more, I guess."

"Don't be frightened by it," Brenda said. "I know it seems like a lot, but it also has forms we will need to use regularly and frequently asked questions."

"Don't worry," I.D. added. "We don't expect you to do more than you can. Pastor Morman has a saying: 'Christ, family, then the church.' While there's plenty to do in this ministry, we never want you or your family to suffer."

"And this ministry is fun!" Brenda said, soothing our worries. "We're going to have a ball together."

"I love having fun," Angenette said. "Sign me up for *allll* of that."

"Yes, please," Mia said. Her bright pink lipstick seemed to match her effervescent spirit.

I could tell that these new acquaintances were just what I needed—what my heart had been longing for.

When Brenda said that Christians could serve and have fun, she lit a light within my soul. I was just beginning to figure out what it meant to live an adventurous, joy-filled life with Christ, but I felt I would learn more as I worked alongside these women who already felt like sisters.

I had no idea Brenda, Mia, Angenette, and I would become the Dare Divas. It seems fitting that our relationship began with an adventure—serving the beautifully diverse group of people at our church. Serving brought so many different people into our lives. There were couples, singles, young people, and seniors, some with financial assets and others who had very little. Each provided insight or wisdom that enriched my life. I had one idea of what friendship could look like, but God wanted to broaden my perspective.

If you're in a season where you're looking for new friends, consider volunteering with your church or a local organization. You might find that it blesses you just as much as it blesses others.

For me, the awakening of meeting new friends came by serving others. Even Mannard found that serving together and forming friendships with other couples at church strengthened our relationship with each other and with God. Working alongside other couples in ministry, we learned we were not alone in the struggles of married life. Those who had been married longer than us gave us advice on putting each other first and balancing the stress of raising kids with loving each other well as husband and wife. We received so many life lessons from individuals we admired and who had allowed the Word of Christ to affect their own lives.

We also had front-row seats to see how God was operating in the lives of his children within the larger church body. As we served, countless individuals and couples blessed our hearts, sometimes in ways we least expected.

When I served in the wedding ministry for a season, I was in my early forties and two other members were in their twenties. One of the women sang in the choir, and I had often admired her vocal abilities. I was surprised when she told me, "One of the reasons I joined the wedding ministry was to get to know you. I wasn't certain just how to do that, but I thought serving alongside you would be a good way to start."

"Same here," said the other young woman, who had married two years earlier and recently welcomed her first child. "I've always admired you and your husband. You two are all about that serving God business."

I was taken aback. I had never imagined people were watching me—so much so that they wanted a closer look. I felt humbled that others looked up to me and wanted to follow my example. I had never viewed myself as a spiritual leader, and yet here God seemed to be opening that door.

●　●　●

Several years after Mannard and I joined the Contact Outreach and Development Ministry, we were asked to take the reins. I enjoyed watching Mannard rise to the challenge in his new role. The kind, compassionate man I had married had a bigger heart than I had even imagined. I marveled at his restraint when dealing with difficult people. He showed me that I should never use my tongue as a weapon. If someone chose to be unkind, I didn't have to reciprocate.

As I watched my husband counsel those who had a grievance with the church, I learned the power of listening and making people feel heard. During our time serving together, I watched Mannard's quiet strength defuse many tensions and bring greater unity to our church body.

I look back on those years serving with Mannard and the Divas as some of my sweetest. Proverbs 27:9 says, "Oil and perfume make the heart glad, and the sweetness of a friend comes from his earnest counsel" (ESV). Through ministry at the church, Mannard and I found earnest counsel that strengthened our relationship. In addition, I found sweetness in the friendships God provided. That sweetness was only amplified as we served hurting people together and witnessed God's glory.

I had once longed for such kinship and soul connection with other women. But before God could grant me the deeper relationships I desired, he planted me in a ministry that would teach me to love people right where they were and show compassion and empathy even when I didn't know how. I prayed with people going through health crises and those at risk of losing their homes. I prayed for restoration in marriages and healing for terminal illnesses. I walked with folks through so many heartaches by offering a hug of understanding, a listening ear to those who felt lost, and words of Scripture to those who felt alone and unloved.

As I served with the Divas, I was amazed to see how each of my friends had their own unique way of showing love. Brenda displayed natural, loving leadership, guiding others

with authority that came from biblical knowledge. Mia grav-
itated toward ministry to children and was attuned to their
innocence. She broke down Scripture to its simplest form—
grace, love, faith—so that even the very young looked up to
her in awe when she explained the mightiness of Christ. And
Angenette was the sassy sister-friend who would have you
giggling one moment and then coming passionately before
the throne of Christ in prayer the next.

As God taught me to be a true friend, I often looked to
Christ, who modeled perfect friendship. He set an unmatched
example of how to love others well. While on earth, he pos-
sessed the characteristics of the truest friend—patient, wise,
kind, loving, self-sacrificing. Jesus could certainly have accomplished his mission alone, but he chose to have friends.
He reached out to the twelve disciples and gave them full ac-
cess to his life. These men became his trusted confidants who
spread the message of salvation to the world. They watched
him do amazing feats such as turning water into wine and
feeding thousands of people with five loaves of bread and
two fish. Jesus's friends had a front-row seat to God's glory
manifesting through him.

In the final hours before he died, Jesus gave his disciples
these instructions: "This is my commandment, that you love
one another as I have loved you. Greater love has no one than
this, that someone lay down his life for his friends" (John
15:12–13 ESV).

At times this command seems so impossible amid busy
schedules and a desire for independence. I can be so wrapped
up in my own life that I forget to put in the time and effort
to get into the messiness of someone else's life, to be there
and love like Jesus loved.

Making new friends and letting them into your heart takes being vulnerable, and if you've been hurt by others in the past, it is not the easiest thing to do. Have you wondered why it has been hard to make friends?

For me, taking a deeper look into my intentions and expectations has eased the way. I've been on many adventures now, but the biggest dare in my life has been to open my heart to others and experience honest, vulnerable relationships. Learning to engage in authentic, imperfect friendships has been one of the most challenging and important lessons I have learned. God has used these friends to expand my heart through joyful and devastating times. I have learned that while God is my rock and foundation, I can lean on other people too.

## AUGUST 2012

As it turns out, the one thing more terrifying than a dare is the horror of real life. I never felt that more strongly than when I drove through the early morning mist behind the ambulance that carried my fifty-year-old husband. There were no sirens echoing through the streets. No lights flashed to warn other drivers to get out of our way. After a catastrophic cardiac event in the early hours of the morning, Mannard had left me. Though I was right there, I had been helpless to save him. My husband was gone.

At the hospital, I watched a nurse pull a sheet over my husband's head. When a hospital attendant came and asked me if I wanted to donate Mannard's eyes and gave me paperwork to fill out, family and friends comforted me. I don't recall who pulled out a tissue to wipe my tears or who brought me a cup of tea. Thankfully, a fellow mom brought Danielle home from cheer camp, as I was too afraid to drive after the shock.

All of a sudden I needed to get out and get some air. I had to leave the horrid room that held my husband's lifeless body. I needed to get out of the hospital and breathe as grief washed over me. Outside, I paced back and forth along the entrance sidewalk, hugging my arms tightly to my body.

Then I saw a figure running toward me from the parking lot. Mia raced my direction with her handbag flopping at her side.

"Sheri!" she screamed, nearly tripping over her own feet. She gathered me into an embrace, and I wept on her shoulder. "What? I . . . I'm trying to breathe, Sheri. Are you? How are you breathing?" Her tears wet my cheek.

Right then, I crumpled. Mia used strong arms to keep me from tumbling to the pavement.

I'm not sure how long we stood there before a car screeched up beside us. Ang stepped out of the passenger side. In her rush to hand the valet her keys, she dropped them. She didn't bother to be courteous as she stepped past the attendant and the keys to get to me and Mia. She didn't say a word or ask any questions. She simply placed her arms around both our necks, forming a circle.

Brenda was on the road at the time, heading to visit her family in New York City. I tried not to worry as she received this news while she was driving. Rapid text messages came from her. I handed my phone to someone—I believe Mia—as I could barely form a sentence, let alone type a text message.

I don't remember everything that happened that morning, but I do remember the prayers. Fervent words that broke into my dark reality like a glimmer of light and connected me to a God who seemed very far away. I'm sure I muted many of those words in that ripe, raw moment. But I leaned into my friends. They stepped in and recited the Word to me. These friends, who *knew* me, forced me to recall all the times in my life when God had made a way out of no way. Even in the pain of my circumstances, I was reminded of all the times God had been faithful to me in the past.

I thought back to falling in love with and marrying my amazing man. I thought of the beautiful life we had built together, raising two healthy children.

Back in the hospital, the confusion and exhaustion washed over me as I collapsed to the ground, right there in the waiting room.

## SEPTEMBER 1977

When I first met Mannard, I was a gangly ten-year-old with neat cornrows in my hair and teeth too large for my mouth. My mom worked in housekeeping at Henry Ford Hospital, and her coworker, Joyce, had a fifteen-year-old son who was on scholarship at an elite private boarding school forty-five minutes away from where we lived. Once, when Joyce was driving him back to school after a weekend in Detroit, she invited my mom and me to tag along.

I folded my skinny legs into the back seat of Joyce's pea-green '72 Ford Thunderbird and shut the door.

"Hey, I'm Mannard."

I turned to see one of the most handsome boys I'd ever laid eyes on sitting next to me. He smiled warmly.

"Hi," I mumbled, wanting to disappear into the leather seat. I didn't feel worthy to be talking to this handsome teenage brainiac.

31

As we drove on windy roads past groves of elm trees and Georgian mansions, Mannard entertained us with stories of his hijinks at boarding school.

I giggled at each story, and soon he had all of us rolling in laughter. I had a huge crush on him, but he wouldn't know that until we started dating eight years later.

## JANUARY 1985

After that magical car ride, I eventually forgot about Mannard and my crush on him. During my senior year of high school, I suddenly began panicking about college. My mom and I had no idea how we would pay for it.

On a crisp, sunny day in January, Mannard appeared at my front door, and my crush came tumbling right back. His mission was to help me with college applications. The funny, daring boy with the Afro had turned into a handsome man. He was six feet tall with a buttery caramel complexion and slightly wavy hair.

"Hi," was all I could muster as Mannard and Joyce stepped through the door. I felt like that tongue-tied ten-year-old kid in the back seat of their car.

"Thanks for helping me," I said, directing Mannard toward the kitchen table where my college forms and financial aid papers were laid out.

"He didn't have a choice," Joyce bellowed from the living room, where she and my mom sat talking.

Mannard folded his jacket neatly across the back of the kitchen chair. He smirked at his mom's comment. "Happy to help, Sheri," he said, his voice just as warm as I remembered.

"All those hours working for free in the financial aid office at school should come in handy."

"You worked for free?" I asked. This strikingly good-looking man was not only brilliant but also a humanitarian?

"Uh, no, wrong word!" He took a seat and removed a calculator and folder from his backpack. "It was work-study, part of my college financial aid package, so I wouldn't need a loan."

"Cool, I could use one of those . . . a work-study." I fluttered my eyelashes, thankful the years had been kind to me. My once-crowded teeth were now neatly stacked without the help of braces, and my long tresses were pressed bone straight midway down my back.

Mannard's eyes pierced mine, and I sensed a mixture of attraction and unease in his gaze as he quickly moved his eyes down to the paperwork. "Well, that's the goal," he said. "There are all kinds of ways to avoid debt—Pell grants, work-study, and . . . uh, the other free one . . ." He struggled for the word.

"Scholarships?" I offered.

"Yeah, yeah, that's it," he said, exhaling deeply.

Was he flustered? Because of *me*?

Two weeks later, I had a school dance and needed a date. "Should I ask him?" I was driving my mom nuts with my quandary about whether or not to ask Mannard to accompany me to the dance. "I mean, he'll say no, right? He graduated from the University of Pennsylvania. That's ivy, Mom. No way he'd want to go to some lame high school dance."

"Oh, goodness, Sheri," Mom said. "Just ask the boy!"

Mannard had been on my mind since the day he helped me. I dialed his number, breathed deeply, and nearly hung up before I heard the tenor of his voice. "Hello?"

I paused. "Hey, Mannard. It's Sheri."

"Sheri!" He said my name so brightly that my heart leapt. "I was just thinking about you."

I giggled. "No you weren't."

"Seriously," he said. "I wanted to ask you to the movies or something."

I was thankful he couldn't see me through the telephone wires, as I was beating my pillow to a pulp with excitement. *Yes, yes, yes!*

"That's funny, 'cause I was thinking about you too," I said. *Don't lose it, Sheri. Keep your calm, girl.* "I kinda need a date for a dance at school."

"Really?" I could hear the smile in his voice. I wasn't imagining it; he liked me.

"I wasn't sure whether to ask because I thought you might be bored," I said, beginning to ramble. "So not sure if you can, or want to, or maybe you're dating someone so she may not like it . . ."

Mannard interrupted my awkward monologue. "No, I'm not dating anyone. And yeah, I'd like to go to the dance with you. When is it? For sure, I'm going with you."

When I hung up, I pranced around my room like I had just won the Miss Universe contest. The man of my dreams had agreed to go on a date with me. *Me.*

Mannard accompanied me to that dance, and after that we were inseparable.

It was easy for me to get hooked on Mannard. He always seemed to anticipate what I needed before I even knew to ask.

When I had poor transportation, he offered to loan me money to buy a used car. When I needed funds for the University of Michigan–Dearborn, he gave me information about scholarships that I applied for and won. He always thought ahead and was knowledgeable about so many things. I was twenty-four when we married in 1991, six years after we began dating.

As a newlywed, all I needed was Mannard. I poured all of my time and attention into my relationship with him. I had friends from high school and college, but I placed those relationships on the back burner.

"Girl, you are turning into a forty-year-old," my college friend Leslie said. "You ain't even twenty-five yet. Let's hit the club!"

I sat at the counter of Leslie's bachelorette pad, sipping a pinot grigio. "I can't go to the club and dance with another man! Please." I tried to ignore the disappointed look on my friend's face. "Hey, if your man danced with another woman, you know you'd throw hot grits at him on the dance floor. And you're not even married!"

"Girl, you're right about that!" she said, laughing. We clinked glasses.

As hard as I tried to keep up the friendships with my single friends, I couldn't connect the way I had before. I'd changed.

As I focused on my husband and eventually my two young children, many of my close female friendships faded away. I would hear about my former girlfriends getting together for girls' nights or exciting weekends in the big city, but I was never invited. And although I may have occasionally been envious, I didn't really mind. I knew in my heart that wasn't me anymore. I was just where I needed to be.

Have you ever felt awkward navigating a new season in your life? When the things we did in our past are no longer attractive, it can be difficult to determine what in our lives has to remain and what has to change.

• • •

On the morning Mannard went to be with the Lord, the first thing that comforted me was these words from Jeremiah: "'For I know the plans I have for you,' declares the LORD, 'plans to prosper you and not to harm you, plans to give you hope and a future'" (29:11). I so wanted to believe that. And my friends were there to assure me that the words were true, even if I couldn't see that through my immediate pain.

When Mannard passed, I was so thankful that God had fulfilled my longing for kinship and close sisterhood through the Dare Divas and fellow ministers of Christ. These weren't quick or uncomplicated relationships. I was still learning to love and be loved by imperfect people. But the richness I experienced, even on the worst day of my life, made every moment of investment worth it.

God had brought people into my life—souls of his making who loved me right where I was—who spoke truth to me and held me on my darkest day. In the months that followed, I would need them desperately. God was already providing for the rough path that lay ahead. That day I had no idea how hard that path would be, and I'm thankful for that. Though the ripple effect of losing Mannard had only just begun, with faithful friends in my life, I knew I was not alone.

# 2

# dare to leap

### if I leap, will you catch me, Lord?

**AUGUST 2014**

Around the second anniversary of Mannard's death, a family friend innocently asked me, "Now that you're past the grief, what are your plans for your remaining years?" Her words hit me like a dagger. Not only did they imply that I was terribly old (I was only forty-seven at the time), but it was as if she was saying that two years was plenty of time to "get over" Mannard's passing and get on with my life—as if I could ever get over Mannard, whom I'd loved since I was eighteen.

I don't know what it means to be fully healed from a loss. When skin is punctured, it will heal over time, first with scabs, then with scars. In many cases, the wound heals so well, no one will ever know the offense occurred. Not so with the soul. These wounds never seem to entirely go away, and I am certain I will feel Mannard's loss for the rest of my life. On days where everything seems to be going well and tragedy is the furthest thing from my mind, something as simple as a song playing on the radio will spark the thought that he is no longer with me. What strikes me the hardest is when the kids have an achievement or major life event and Mannard's not there to see it. Their dad, who adored them and showed them constant love and acceptance, is gone. Even though the worst of the grieving has passed, there will always be moments when the wound still feels fresh.

Before Mannard's death, Angenette, Brenda, Mia, and I tackled numerous dares. But the first dare after Mannard's death was something that would truly push me to my limits and require me to trust in God in a way I never had before.

To put it simply, I thought my friends were nuts. Skydiving, in my mind, was not for someone like me. The Sheri I knew was quiet, reserved, and cautious and would definitely *never ever* voluntarily hurl herself out of a moving plane, especially as the sole parent and provider of two children. Leaping from an aircraft thousands and thousands of feet above the earth, with a nylon parachute as the only line of defense between death and landing on the ground safely, seemed beyond brave. It was the edge of pure lunacy.

The four of us were huddled in my family room one afternoon, our various shades of brown legs curled up on my sofa and chairs, mugs of coffee in our hands. We were taking some time to reconnect about our families, careers, and world events when, to my horror, Angenette brought up her idea for our next dare: skydiving.

"I tell you, the plunge is amazing," she said. "It's so much better than a roller coaster." She aimed those words at me, knowing my love of coasters and fear of skydiving. Angenette, who had skydived six years earlier, found the experience thrilling and had been actively trying to recruit us to join her in doing it again.

I took a gulp of coffee, sank further into my chair, and rolled my eyes to the ceiling.

Brenda spoke up. "I'm kinda afraid of heights. Why not a bicycling trip or something? I'm good with anything that keeps us on the ground."

"I second that!" I said. Brenda and I clinked coffee mugs. "If there's a mishap with a coaster, you usually live to tell the tale. Can't say the same about a parachute gone bad."

"Yeah, things can go wrong," Mia began, "but that's true of all the dares. Heck, it's true of driving a car! I think I'd like to try it anyway." This from the same girl who'd gotten stuck dangling hundreds of feet in the air during our zip-lining dare.

Ang nodded in agreement as Mia continued. "If we are going to call ourselves the Dare Divas, then we should be *daring*! I mean, cycling? Big whoop! We've all been riding bikes since we were little. No offense, Brenda."

Brenda gave a lackluster smile, and I sighed at the direction this conversation was headed.

I did think about what I'd miss if I didn't do the dare. I'd miss out on bragging rights, the unity of accomplishing a death-defying challenge with the Divas, and the sense of pride that came from being afraid but doing it anyway. I finally decided that my God was bigger than my fears, even though I wasn't absolutely sure I wouldn't go *splat* during the dare.

I called up Ang later and gave her my vote. "I'm in."

●  ●  ●

The irony of deciding to skydive while I was free-falling in my personal life was not lost on me. A week before the jump, I was particularly racked with anxiety as my real estate attorney outlined my options for the house. Due to poor financial management following Mannard's death, our mortgage was now underwater in a particularly dismal economy. To make matters worse, a business deal Mannard had entered before his death had suddenly gone bad, spiraling into a costly lost investment. And the person I always turned to for knowledge, expertise, and comfort was gone. I did the only thing I knew to do at that point: I got on my knees at the side of my bed.

I sobbed and sobbed, tears streaming down my face, my nose running like a faucet. I had made costly, silly mistakes before, but now there was no partner to balance my faults, no one to act as my parachute when I needed to be bailed out.

With my dry ebony knees chafing on my throw rug, I thanked God for his grace and asked Jesus to forgive me for depending more on Mannard's guidance and provision than his. "Lord," I prayed, "I'm humbling myself before you. I know that I have not always recognized you as the source of my blessings. I have been prideful and falsely believed that others could make a way for me more than you could. Forgive me. Jesus, I need you, not just to help me out of messes, but to guide me and use me to be what you feel is best for this life. Please give me wisdom and peace as I move forward. Amen."

I so wanted to make sure that my steps aligned with Christ. I also wanted to reassure my kids that all was okay, though in the beginning, I hid my grief. I muffled my sobs in my pillowcase at bedtime, cried in solitude in the shower, and when alone, shouted through the house, hair askew and wild.

With the continuation of the dares, I desired to shake myself up, get myself to believe that if I could master things that frightened me outside my home, I could master things that gave me anxiety at home as well. I found that meditating on the words of Christ helped me to see myself not as invincible but as mighty, able to tackle all things, even frightening things.

When I'd first told the kids about the jump in May, they seemed to be on board.

"Sure, Mom." Danielle smiled.

"Cool," David said, giving me a thumbs-up.

Turns out they were both so enthralled with their phones at the time, what I was saying hadn't sunk in. In July, three days before the jump, I brought it up again.

I was making breakfast and actually feeling amped about the upcoming challenge. "The girls and I are going to make a big day of the jump," I said, piling pancakes on their plates. "We're doing a picnic at Skydive Tecumseh before we jump, then dinner at Champps after." Considering my earlier reservation, I was pretty impressed with my newfound bravery. I assumed I'd be rewarded with pride from my children. Instead they both looked at me in shock.

"You are *seriously* going to do it?" Danielle asked.

David shook his head. "Crazy. All of y'all."

"Mom, you're our *only* parent," Danielle said. "Do you think it's a good idea?"

David shoved a forkful of pancakes in his mouth. "She's done crazy dares before."

"Nothing like this!" Danielle screeched. "She could . . . she could . . . *die*!"

"Danielle has a point, Mom," David said. "It is pretty risky."

41

My joy departed as I looked at my children's worried faces. "If you don't want me to go, I won't," I said.

Facing my kids, I felt deflated but mostly foolish. Maybe it *was* selfish to even think about doing this. Their father had died only twenty-four months before. And they were nowhere close to getting over that loss. I knew even when the pain was hidden or masked, it was always there, just beneath the surface.

Danielle's eyes looked teary as she intertwined my hand with hers. "I don't want to be afraid, Mom. Can you promise me it will be okay?"

*Promises. Promise to love you forever. Until death do us part.*

As I gazed at my child, I knew what she wanted. It was the same thing I wanted from Christ. She wanted me to give her the absolute assurance that all would be well with the world and we wouldn't suffer again the way we had when Mannard died. Oh, how I wanted to give her that. And I felt I could that day. All I had to do was decline the dare.

"Danielle, Mom can't promise you she'll live forever," David said.

I looked at him, amazed at the strength and wisdom coming from my child.

"You know what happened with Dad. There are no guarantees."

"But there's a difference between dying naturally of a heart attack and risking your life for fun," Danielle said.

"I can't say I completely get it, these crazy dares," David said, "but I want her to enjoy life." He turned to me. "I'm okay with it."

Danielle sat silently, looking down at her uneaten food.

I took her hands in mine. "We all want to live long, happy lives, but there's no way to go about living without risks. We just have to try our hardest to get it right and hope for the best."

"I guess the other dares have worked out," Danielle said reluctantly. "I can't say I'm not scared, but I will support you."

"Great!" David leapt up from his chair. "Now that we're good, can I jump too?"

"No!" Danielle and I barked in unison.

"Wait, what? What about all the 'taking risks' and 'trying our hardest' stuff you just said?"

I didn't want to squelch my son's eagerness to try something daring himself, but I stood firm. "You don't have the money to pay your way. If you want to skydive after you've finished college and done some things with your life—and can afford it—I'll support you. But this is not your day."

"Right!" Danielle said to him, brushing past his shoulder. "Stay in your own lane."

In defeat, David marched toward the family room. "Well, if I can't jump, I won't watch."

I didn't fight David or make him support me. It would have been pointless. Besides, I saw my son's underlying fear. Even if he didn't recognize it himself, I knew. He had seen one parent die; why chance seeing that again?

●　●　●

Two days before the jump, I visited my mom. After my conversation with my kids, I had decided not to jump after all. It just wasn't worth it to me to risk putting them through any additional trauma if something went wrong.

"I'll just sit this dare out," I said. I sat next to my mother on the sofa. I knew she'd be supportive of this decision. She had never been pleased about the idea of me skydiving.

"Can't say I'm totally sorry about it," she said.

As my mother's only child, I enjoyed our daily talks, even when we didn't agree. "I guess I was being selfish even thinking about it." I grabbed a throw pillow and hugged it tight.

"Listen, it's a dream," she said. "Your dream. It's good to feel the blood flowing through your veins."

"Yeah, but I have kids. Kids who lost their dad."

"Okay."

"And, they'll feel better if I don't."

"Okay," she said again, a smirk starting to form on her face.

"So, I'm not doing it."

"Okay." She raised her eyebrows.

"Is that all you have to say?" I huffed.

"Well, I was wondering if you're also going to give up jogging." Mom ruffled the pages of the *Detroit Free Press* like she hadn't said anything unusual.

"What?" I asked, becoming more irritated by the second.

"Oh, and cycling. I know you love it, but it's got to go."

"Mom!"

"And those walks with your neighbors—nix them," she said. "You're a mom, sweetie. Better safe than sorry."

I lightheartedly tossed the pillow toward her. She always had a special way of making me laugh, even when I didn't know what to do.

Mom chuckled. "Baby, you can get run down by a car while you're walking across the street. You can be at the wrong place at the wrong time. All sorts of harm can come to you just by living. But, honey, you have to *live*. Do you really think you're teaching the kids that you can guarantee your safety by locking yourself away from any kind of danger?"

She moved closer and cupped my chin. "Are you going to spend the rest of your life saying no to any opportunity that might be risky? I know Mannard wouldn't want that for you. You can't play it safe your whole life. Most people live after jumping out of airplanes, baby. And many people simply die in their own beds."

I fell into my mother's arms, her sweater muffling my cry.

"When it's time, Jesus will call us all home," she said. "We don't determine the place or day, nor do we lengthen our time here by playing it safe. Now go on and show your kids—show all of us—how to live."

•  •  •

On the drive to the skydiving site near Ann Arbor, Michigan, Danielle and I shared the ride in a happy silence. The mood was no longer heavy from our family talk. It was a nearly cloud-free day, and nothing but expectation and excitement hung in the air.

"Wow, look at that," Danielle said, pointing out the window. One parachute after another landed after a skydiving jump. "I still can't believe you're going to do that, Mom."

As we pulled into the parking lot, I shut off the motor. "You are more important to me than the dares, Danielle. Just say the word and I'll watch today. I can do it another time . . . or maybe not." I grinned and shook my head, secretly hoping that Danielle would be my out.

She smiled back. "No, go ahead. I'm glad there are a bunch of us here. I wouldn't want to be the only one watching. Are you a little scared?"

"I'm a *lot* scared. But maybe if I do this, I won't be so afraid in other areas of my life."

Danielle nodded, and we got out of the car.

At Skydive Tecumseh, there were picnic tables in an area for supporters and onlookers to set up lunch. That's where the Divas were—all fired up, laughing and smiling like they were about to cheer for the Detroit Lions instead of launching themselves out of an airplane.

Mia and her posse, about eight people, were there, along with Angenette and one of her friends, Brenda and her two kids, and Danielle and me.

Just as Danielle and I settled in, Mia corralled us for our Dare Diva picture. Her delight was, as always, contagious. Photographs and selfies helped to distract us from the great plunge to come.

It was an ideal day to jump: warm, no fog, no rain, and just enough clouds to keep the sun from blazing. The skydive crew on the ground made preparations for the flight in a barnlike structure where our one-hour training would begin.

I had three options as a first-time skydiver: (1) learn to skydive solo, without an instructor, like a wannabe Rambo or Navy SEAL; (2) learn to control the parachute and land with limited aid from instructors, likely plummeting both of us to our deaths; or (3) have a certified professional with hundreds of jumping hours to guide, direct, and deploy both parachutes while I tagged along. I chose option 3: tandem skydiving.

The flight suits weren't nearly as sexy as we'd imagined. They were blue, lumpy, misshapen cotton with "Property of Skydive Tecumseh" printed like a badge where a left breast pocket would be. (As if anyone would *want* to steal those ugly things.) There were no *Top Gun* aviator glasses and no helmets. I'll say that again: NO HELMETS?

My tandem instructor, Curt, chuckled at my inquiry. "If you crash at 125 miles per hour, a plastic hard-shell helmet ain't gonna help. A helmet will just contain the brain matter."

Lovely.

Curt must have seen the dread on my face, because he cupped my shoulder with a firm hand. "Look, we're gonna have a real good time up there. Everything will be fine, and you're gonna be so doggone proud afterward."

I nodded, but only to distract myself from puking after his graphic description of brain matter.

"I've been doing this for some time," Curt continued, not sensing that silence would have been golden at this point. "Flew in the Navy and—"

"See, Sheri?" Ang chimed in. "We have experts, professionals who have done this for a living. We are going to have a ball!"

As the flight crew directed us to board, our posse of family and friends cheered us on.

"You've got this!" Danielle shouted.

I hugged my daughter tight. At seventeen, she allowed me to squeeze her in a way she had carefully avoided since the first day of middle school.

"Have fun, Mom," she said. "I'll see you when you land."

I had no words. I gave her a thumbs-up and walked to the airplane. Brenda would board behind me. Angenette and Mia had already boarded with their instructors. I was grateful I wasn't alone.

As the plane ascended, I inhaled deeply and prayed silently. *I am more than a conqueror. I can do all things through Christ who sustains me. God is my protector.*

"We are doing this," Ang shouted over the engine noise. "We are doing this *together*!"

I turned to see Mia smiling broadly. "I knew we'd all step up and do it. My knees are quaking, though."

I forced a smile. "I can believe *you ladies* are doing it. I'm still in shock that *I* am, though!"

We all laughed.

Ang, the seasoned one who had jumped before, was so confident and reassuring—that gave me hope. "No turning back now!" she said, nudging me.

"Don't think so?" I replied. I knew my options. I could still refuse to jump and could sit back happily as the girls leapt without me.

"No. Turning. Back." Mia's eyes curled up to match her smile. "I wonder if everyone below will know it's us when we get close to touch down?"

"Probably not," Ang said. "Not until they see our little brown faces."

Brenda was way up front while Mia and I sat on the edge of our seats in the middle. Ang settled in at the back of the aircraft seat like she was readying herself for a massage.

"Too bad we can't do that circular formation in the air with our hands locked," Mia said. "Wouldn't that be so cool?" She was referring to the specialty dive team move we had seen in the Skydive Tecumseh literature. No way did we have the experience, skill, or ability to do that. Not now, not ever.

Angenette snickered. "We can save that for the next jump."

48

"You two better stop messing with me," I said. This was not the time; my nerves were already frayed. I turned around and stepped up the intensity of my praying.

I visualized exactly how this dare, how this dream of mine, would go. I would soar; I would fly through the air and the heavens with delight. I would live to tell all who cared to hear about it.

Within five minutes, as the aircraft reached the jump point, the Holy Spirit answered my prayer and my nerves eased a bit. Though I was not completely calm, I wasn't losing my mind either.

Brenda would be the first to jump, which wasn't the plan.

"I thought I was supposed to be the last to jump!" she screamed after receiving word from the crew that she would be first. She complied—reluctantly. She stood from her seat and shuffled like a shackled inmate toward the exit door, attached to her tandem partner.

She was supposed to be last; she'd made us promise. She had developed a slight phobia of heights over the years and wasn't too keen to do the dare in the first place. But she had to go first since her tandem guide had been held up from a prior jump and the two were the last to enter our plane. "Last in, first out," he said, and patted Brenda's shoulder. She gave a loud whimper and looked back forlornly.

Normally, the three remaining Divas would have laughed it off as an "oh well" moment, but we were silent. If Ang and Mia were like me, they were thankful not to be the first to go.

Suddenly it dawned on me that I would be next. An ache grew quickly in the pit of my stomach, and I willed myself not to get sick before it was my turn to jump.

As her partner rocked them back and forth at the exit door, the auburn-brown streaks in Brenda's hair shone and her tresses blew wildly. Then the back of her partner's blue jumpsuit blew out of the plane like a piece of paper—*swoosh*. It was that quick. I didn't hear a peep out of Brenda.

"Ok, Eagle, time to take flight," Curt said, nudging me to get up. His tone shifted to business mode. "Remember everything I told you?"

"Yeah, yeah." I nodded much too quickly, then put my pride aside. "Tell me again."

"Just remember to keep your arms pointed in front of you, hands flat," he said. "I got the rest. Remember, enjoy it!"

As my feet dangled over the edge of a Beechcraft King aircraft some fourteen thousand feet above ground, I began to feel my heart race from both excitement and pure fear. The wind blew vigorously, and the only thing between me and a haphazard tumble out of the plane was the tether attached to my tandem guide, who was anchored solidly to the aircraft. Beyond me, clouds enveloped the aircraft— beautiful, yet difficult to fully enjoy because of what was about to come.

I would have gifted him with a smile at his attempt to comfort me, but there was solid ground below that could turn my body into mush if this dare went bad.

Then it happened.

I surrendered. I looked back toward Curt, sighed deeply, and collected myself to breathe shallow breaths. "Let's do it," I said. "I'm ready."

Within seconds I was dropping like a boulder, gravity forcibly jetting me to earth. I felt weightless, a mere feather in the universe.

The fall wasn't like a roller coaster as Ang had shared earlier—the feeling that your stomach is topsy-turvy and you may hurl at any minute. Instead, it felt like I was on a fast-moving lateral conveyor belt, like I was being speed-trekked through a vigorous wind tunnel. With the gusts flapping at my eyes, I could only see clouds of space and couldn't make out any images. I was moving like a bullet through time, and I imagine that the feeling is like being in the vortex of a hurricane.

My sole thought through the initial plunge was, *Oh Lord, please help me land safe and sound, and can I breathe?*

The initial plunge lasted about twenty seconds, but it felt like a good ten minutes before the first parachute activated. Out of nowhere, a man with a camera came up to me and snapped my picture.

Along with our tandem guides, each Dare Diva had her own personal photographer to capture midair moments. As Curt focused on getting us to land safely, Jeff, my photographer, worked to capture great shots.

Jeff floated toward me midair, coming close enough to nudge my hands. I stifled a smile. He snapped. Jeff frowned and gave me a thumbs-down like I had failed *him*, then he jetted to land.

It was when the second parachute deployed that the magic began. At that point we were some nine thousand feet from the ground. I was mesmerized.

"Beautiful, ain't it?" Curt whispered with wonder, as though this was his first jump.

"Yes. Yes, it is," I said.

Within seconds I went from abject terror to magnificent bliss.

It is a wonder how those horrific life events seem to never end, that the trials last much longer than we think we can bear. Wouldn't it be a beautiful thing if during those gut-wrenching times, I could transition my thinking to the other side of dread and anxiety instead of allowing fear to consume me? If only I could reach for joy and channel peace when I'm at my most vulnerable.

The violent wind had turned into a calm breeze that kissed my face, and my body relaxed. *This must be what birds feel like*, I thought.

I saw cities far below and farmland that looked like heaps of dirt. As we floated closer to the earth, the picture of God's creation became clearer and more precise. I could make out circular lakes and tiny matchbox-size rooftops. I could see other skydivers landing below me and our group cheering their safe landing. My myopic vantage point had widened, and soon everything that was once unclear was razor sharp.

My vantage point had changed. It was no longer fraught with fear but filled with delight.

As Curt and I touched down, we literally slid across earth as though it was home plate at a Tigers baseball game.

Once our tandem partners unstrapped and headed to their next jumps, we four Divas embraced in a circle, a celebration of friendship, love, and the fact we all landed safely. We hugged tightly, and none of us were in any hurry to let go.

In the distance, I saw Danielle smiling widely. I smiled back and gave her a jubilant thumbs-up.

As parents, we are forever teaching our children even when they become full-fledged adults. The one thing I want my children to see is that I am always moving toward being happy, whole, and courageous.

. . .

During my childhood and up until Mannard's death, my faith had never been truly tested. Now, each day my belief in a higher power and the loving relationship that I work toward understanding has become the epicenter of sustaining me through crucial elements of life and everyday living. What I've learned in addition to developing my faith is that sometimes you have to leave your problems at home and live.

In my daily devotional, the poet Gertrude Stein was quoted as saying, "Considering how dangerous everything is, nothing is really frightening." In essence, life and existing on earth are fraught with unknown dangers. And yet God instructs us to move forward with passion and faith.

I know there will be times when I'm afraid. There will be times in my personal life when I'll want to stay stagnant because acting, moving forward, is frightening. There are so many unknowns, with possibilities of complete failure and even my own demise.

It's those free falls in life that make me wonder what God is up to.

When all is awry, when I can't breathe, when I can't see clearly, and when I am trying desperately to survive, then I question God's very existence and the depth of his concern for us. *Why me? Will I be okay? If you love me, why did you let this happen? Can I trust you again? Will you allow something sinister, something evil, to happen to me or my loved ones again?*

The opposite is true during those times of peace and calm when all is going well in my life. There are no questions. I'm too busy enjoying the ride.

When I am afraid, I must remember that God's grace, like that parachute, is activated in my life. It doesn't mean that I will not have periods of anguish or problems or losses, and there may even be times when I suffer.

Those are all by-products of our existence on earth. We do not live in Eden, and this planet is not heaven. But God has given me his word that through it all—the deep plunges and the soaring heights—he has me. And I will be okay. I will be more than okay; I will be his.

# 3

# dare to trust

### zip-lining toward peace

When a person dies, it's like an earthquake. The main event violently shakes you, but there are always lingering aftershocks. When my husband died suddenly that rainy August morning, his passing shook many people—neighbors, colleagues, friends—but it leveled those at the epicenter: me and my children. My son was there when his father died; he could do nothing to stop it. My daughter learned of his passing on social media as she came home from cheerleading camp. In the wake of Mannard's death, we could barely comprehend—let alone accept—that he was gone.

The question that plagued me was *why*. Why him? At the hospital, as I watched the nurse pull the sheet over Mannard's body, a hollowness crept over me. This was real. There was no divine explanation for why my vibrant, loving husband had died at age fifty, when his family needed him so badly.

I was deeply hurt. I was angry. I was ticked at a God who I thought had abandoned me.

I'd attended church since I was a young girl. And I believed in God. But in that moment, I wanted to have a sit-down conversation with the Almighty. He had made a mistake! Looking back, I can't believe my audacity—to think that I, one of his creations, had the right to tell God off because of his bad decision.

In those first hours, our house was full of people waiting on me. They brought me cups of coffee and put cushions under my feet. When they asked me if I was okay, I lied and told them I was fine. I couldn't allow myself the luxury of losing it and sharing how I really felt. I was terrified of letting people see the shattered, crumbling woman I'd become overnight. I thought I needed to remain strong for those depending on me: my children, my mother, my mother-in-law. So that first night, and for many nights to come, I cried quietly with the door closed in the bed where Mannard had died.

After the first few weeks, the number of people checking in on me slowed down from a flood to a trickle. I didn't blame them. People had their own lives, jobs, and families. I'm sure many people would have welcomed me calling, crying, and processing my fears with them, but I was quickly slipping into depression. I started believing the lies that no one cared—that I wasn't worthy of care.

Along with the Divas, other friends and family had come to the hospital, and in the week after Mannard's death, each of them came to my house. They delivered groceries, washed my dishes, and offered their shoulders to cry on. But I never disclosed the worst to them. I couldn't bring myself to share my darkest thoughts for fear that they would see my morbid thinking as a sign that I was an unfit mother. I had worked so hard to keep up the perfect family image—the clean house, the strong marriage, the well-adjusted kids. I felt like the jig was up. With Mannard gone, it would be clear that he had been the provider, the stronger half of our duo. I couldn't let anyone see how broken I'd been all along.

Hiding my imperfections from others had become the norm, a mask I wore to hide my pride that I wasn't Superwoman after all. Maybe you've worn these masks before and can relate.

Though I had been in the church since I was a child, my faith had never weathered any major storms. My life with Mannard had been extremely comfortable, and I had little real-world practice in trusting God through trials. Mannard's sudden passing cast doubt on everything I believed. I couldn't trust in good health or the promise of a long life. Though I had prayed that Mannard would live, the opposite had happened.

All the preexisting notions I had about God began to unravel. The uncertainty of his very nature left me perplexed. God had changed on me overnight. I lived a good life, had a good marriage, and served at church. Deep down I knew that my happiness wasn't a result of the good things I was doing, but my efforts seemed to be paying off: my marriage was intact, our children were thriving, and we were all healthy.

My doubts about God took me to a dark place. After weeks of extreme insomnia and relentless anxiety, I was certain that I would not survive Mannard's death. I went to the doctor, who prescribed Xanax. That night I slept better than I had in three years, catching up on weeks of sleep all at once, it seemed. My tranquilizers got rid of the pesky, jittery tinge in my skin that kept me on edge most days. My embarrassment over losing the contents of my stomach on a neighbor's shoes, my worry over how to pay our bills on time, the crushing loneliness I felt lying down in our huge four-poster bed at night—all of that vanished.

When my one-month supply was gone, my physician cut me off. "The pills aren't meant to be a lifestyle, Sheri," he said with a mix of concern and pity. "They can't magically make your grief disappear. I prescribed them to get you past the first weeks of shock so you could cope with what's ahead. You still need to do the necessary work to overcome this. It's going to take time, not pills."

I shrugged off his suggestion to see a therapist. I didn't need psychoanalysis. I just needed the pills. I was weighed down by all of the secrets I was keeping from my family, medical professionals, and even the Divas. I felt ashamed. I was certain that I could not handle the weight of my life without Mannard.

When I ran out of prescription drugs, I turned to alcohol. Vodka was my liquor of choice because it looked like water. I found I could hide the results of my drinking by imbibing alone inside the confines of my home. When I fell out of my bathtub headfirst, no one was there to see my bloody nose or chipped tooth. The alcohol calmed my nerves, but it couldn't fill the void my husband's death left. It could only offer a cheap, temporary escape that never actually made me feel better.

Drinking put me into a deep slumber, but I still had horrific nightmares I couldn't wake from no matter how hard I tried. With every morning came a blazing hangover. Many days I was in no shape to report to my job as a marketing specialist. I would call off work simply because I couldn't get out of bed. I was the queen of excuses. I had a migraine, or my car battery was dead, or a skunk sprayed me while I was taking out the trash. I had a sympathetic boss, but finally even she gave me an ultimatum: "Get your act together, Sheri, or we'll have to put you on probation."

When in trouble, even Christians can find themselves in the midst of substance abuse. Satan likes to hurl this shame in our faces to tell us we're unworthy. Have you ever found yourself in a place like this?

● ● ●

My wake-up call came several months later when I tumbled off my back deck after one too many cranberry vodkas and sprained my ankle. It was the last of many signs that I needed to straighten out my act. While I had been dependent on prescription drugs and alcohol to numb my pain in the months since Mannard's death, my destructive habits had not yet crossed into full-blown addiction. Still, I realized if I didn't make changes, there would be even greater consequences.

The next day, I gathered the unfinished and unopened vodka bottles and drove them across town to my friend Lisa's house. I was still too embarrassed to tell the Divas about what was going on, but Lisa, a high school friend, had seen me at my worst throughout the years. In that moment, I felt she was the one person I could trust.

When I arrived with the box of two half-finished handles of Grey Goose and a fresh Ketel One bottle, Lisa had no idea of the nature of my demons. "What's this?" She laughed. "Are we having a party?"

"No, I'm making you my accountability partner," I said, pushing past her to put my spoils on her granite countertop. "I think I may have a problem. I need to stop, and I need your help."

My strength disappeared, and I broke down in tears, telling Lisa all of the sordid details of the hell I'd been living. She embraced me and vowed to help. For the next few months, she made house calls almost every day, showing love and understanding while also scouring my cabinets for spirits. It took a while, but I began to see a pinhole of light breaking through the clouds of my despair.

Coming clean about our addictions, weaknesses, and despair aids us in getting the help we need. If you don't have that one friend to turn to, there are mental health resources in your city and state to aid you. Asking for help is showing strength.

●    ●    ●

About a year after I stopped drinking, God gave me a clearer picture of what he had done. In the summer of 2014, the Divas and I set off on an adventure, another dare. Although two years had passed since Mannard's death, it still felt like we'd just kissed good night the night before. I hadn't embraced the "new normal," and I wondered if I ever would.

Our five-hour zip-line experience wound us through the forests of West Virginia along beautiful, meandering paths with breathtaking views of rock formations and the New River Gorge. The course challenged our stamina with steady climbs up to platforms that hovered four hundred feet above the ground. There were several times the Divas and I had to stop to catch our breath—sometimes from lack of physical endurance, sometimes from fear, and sometimes from the gorgeous sights that awaited us around each bend. At each landing, a series of ropes and harnesses ensured no one plummeted to the bottom. The Divas and I had zip-lined a few years earlier, during a girls' weekend in northern Michigan. God only knows why we decided to zip-line in the dead of winter in one of the coldest parts of the country, and I still have vivid memories of the frigid air whipping across my face and the intense tingling in my nose when I finally thawed out after hours of numbness. I loved every second of it.

But that was *before* Mannard passed away. Despite being four hundred feet in the air and over four hundred miles away from home, I was slapped with the realization that every memory would now be divided into two eras—"before" and "after." My husband would not be there to welcome me home this time or to give me a congratulatory high five before pulling me into his arms. As I walked along the trail, I wondered how I could find the same joy without Mannard—both in this dare and in my life.

A rickety wooden bridge came into view, snapping me out of my reverie. It swayed wildly in the wind and looked like it might burst into pieces at any moment. Our guides, Hugh and Molly, tried to alleviate our fears by jumping on the planks like little kids on a bed. I held tightly to the ropes that served as railings, trying not to hyperventilate as I looked down at the river hundreds of feet below us.

"Please stop," Mia moaned, looking as green as the forest canopy around us.

"Cut it out," Angenette demanded, hustling across the bridge as fast as possible. "Let's get on with it, shall we?"

On the other side of the bridge, we began a steep ascent up roughly hewn steps to our first zip of the day. When we saw the lay of the land, I'm sure our four jaws dropped in unison. The line dove straight down for at least fifty feet before leveling off, which meant hurling ourselves off the plank and into a free fall. There would be no easing into it.

Having been so eager to cross the bridge, Angenette was naturally up first. She carefully sat down on the platform, allowing her feet to dangle over the edge. "I can't believe I'm doing this!" she said, glancing back at us with a smile that betrayed her nerves.

Boulders and a tangle of jagged branches lay five hundred feet below. What if she jumped and something went wrong? The marketing material had advertised the company's pristine safety record, but the five pages of waivers we had to sign seemed to tell a different story.

Ang looked over the edge to get a better view of the drop below. "Girl, I thought we agreed to zip-line, *not* bungee jump," she said, eyeing our guide skeptically.

Molly smiled. "It does get easier. This is the most challenging one—then easy breezy."

Ang offered a half smile. "As an attorney, I guess I really *do* need to read the fine print next time." She looked forward, leaning into the harness as she pushed off the platform. I heard her scream—first in fear, then in glee—as she plummeted down the line.

Brenda bravely stepped up to go next and got into position on the plank. Ten seconds passed. Then twenty.

"Time to make your move, Brenda," Molly said. "We can't wait here forever."

Brenda winced. "I'm going to do it," she said, shaking her rope with conviction and scooting forward slightly. After a few more seconds, she looked back with resignation. "I can't do it. Just push me."

Molly knelt beside Brenda, gently placing a hand on her back. "Are you sure?"

"Yes, just do it. But don't count. I'm going to sit here and—"

Before Brenda could complete her instructions, Molly gave her a solid shove, sending her flying. Soon Brenda was on the other side, smiling and waving alongside Angenette.

Mia and I looked at one another.

"You're up next!" Mia said, smirking and stepping two paces back. "You've done zips before. You've got this!" She was using the same sweet-talking sales pitch that had gotten us into this mess. Even though she's an auditor, I swear the woman could sell snow in Switzerland.

Rolling my eyes at her, I breathed in deep and did a little motivational dance, which basically involved me flapping my arms like a chicken and bouncing on my toes as I willed myself not to die. Molly quickly put a stop to my shenanigans and placed the zip rope firmly in my hands.

I sat down and said a quick prayer before leaning into the rope and inching my hips off the plank. The fall was similar to the initial dive of a roller coaster. I heard a Tarzan-like scream emerge from my mouth. Finally, the pulley engaged to level me out, and for a moment I was totally free as I flew toward the platform: free of pain, free of sorrows, free of the heavy burdens of the future. In that moment, I was at peace and taken with the thrill of being alive.

Once Mia joined us on the other side, we began walking to the next zip. Having survived the previous death-defying drop, I felt confident that this zip would be a cakewalk.

"We have a surprise for you," Molly announced, arching her eyebrows mischievously as we arrived at the platform. "This zip is rigged so that two people can jump off at the same time and race alongside each other to the other side. Anyone interested?"

Even though we're all friends, we Divas have a severe competitive streak. We call each other "sister-friends" for a reason, and that description definitely extends to good-natured sibling rivalry.

After the challenge was issued, Ang was the first to volunteer. "I'll happily take on my fellow Diva," she said, flexing her bicep.

"Bring it!" Brenda said, stepping up to face Ang. "Stop the chatter and get ready to have your tail whooped."

Mia and I laughed, preparing to watch this epic Dare Diva duel. Ang and Brenda launched off the plank. They seemed to move in unison, and it was difficult to see who was ahead. When both were safe on the other side, it was clear Ang had won from the way she was jumping around, as though she'd just caught the game-winning touchdown at the Super Bowl.

Mia and I were up next, encouraged by how easy and fun the other two had made it look. We got into position and screamed the special catchphrase that always bolstered our courage when a big obstacle lay ahead: "Dare Divas activate!"

We pushed off, zooming toward the plank on the other side of the deep ravine. We laughed and hollered as Ang and Brenda cheered us on.

All of a sudden, Mia started to slow down as I raced ahead.

*Yes!* I thought. *I'm gonna win this one!* But when I reached the plank, Brenda and Angenette were still looking behind me. Their expressions told me something was wrong—very wrong. I turned to see Mia dangling in midair about halfway across the line. She was stuck.

"What happened?" I asked.

"They don't know," Brenda said, eyes glued on Mia.

A few extra crew members were already rushing over to help. Molly and Hugh gathered ropes and discussed how to bring Mia safely back to the plank.

I locked my gaze on my friend as if the act alone would keep her safe, keep her from dropping four hundred feet to the rock-strewn ravine below. She appeared to be snug in her harness, but any malfunction would mean serious injury—or worse.

"What's your friend's name?" a crew member asked, interrupting my anxious thoughts.

"Mia," I said. "Mia Lewis."

The woman raised a megaphone to her mouth. "Hey Mia, you okay out there?"

"Yes, I'm fine," Mia shouted.

"You are going to be okay," the woman said in a calm voice. "We're going to come and get you. You're going to be just fine."

I looked at Brenda and Angenette. We all stood there helplessly.

"What went wrong?" Angenette asked a crew member standing nearby.

"Not sure," he said. "It could be the pulley, or maybe a wire rope clip got jammed. We'll find out once we get her to the plank."

Molly put on a harness and walked over to the zip line,

a mass of rope tied in a loop around her left shoulder. She confidently hoisted herself to the wire and wrapped her arms and legs over it like a sloth hanging from a tree. We all stood in hushed silence and watched as Molly begin to inch across the wire.

"I'm coming to get you, Mia!" Molly said, her voice bright, masking any worries she may have had about Mia's safety or her own.

Mia was yards away. While I couldn't see her face, it wasn't hard to imagine what it would feel like to be stranded, dangling high above the ground. I turned to Brenda and Angenette and noticed that they had their eyes closed in prayer. In that moment, praying was the only thing we could do for our friend.

The wait for Molly to ease Mia back to the platform was agonizing, but a look at my watch revealed that the whole ordeal had only been ten minutes from beginning to end. Using a series of clamps and ropes, Hugh slowly reeled Mia and Molly back to the platform until they were within reach of the other guides. As soon as Mia's feet hit the plank and they disengaged her from the wire, we Divas piled on, giving her the biggest group hug of her life.

When you're going through a trial, does the wait for a breakthrough seem excruciating? It has been for me; it was for Mia.

It turned out that Mia's wire clip had gotten jammed. Despite all the checks and double checks the crew had performed before we started our day, we encountered an unexpected bump in the road and were left shaken.

During times of uncertainty, we must hang in there; do our part by praying, actively pursuing life, and daring to look head-on at the scary thing; and patiently be assured that help is coming.

There have been many times in my own life when I felt I was left hanging, when the pitfalls and obstacles I had feared still happened despite all my prior planning. Mannard's passing was no exception. With his death, it felt as if God had taken away my safety net in one fell swoop, leaving me with no support system and no way to cope.

Yet in the wake of this dare, I came to realize that God was using this tumultuous season to awaken a new life within me. Something had to die in *me* so he could transform my life into what he desired it to be—and that thing ended up being my dependency on Mannard. After Mannard's death, the Lord had to remind me—sometimes gently and sometimes painfully—that he is the one I should depend on and seek out when I need help.

As scary as Mia's experience was for us all, I came back from our adventure with something a bit more unexpected: peace. The simple joy of living that I found during each zip helped me to reconnect with that part of myself that could truly find happiness in the simplest of things. I realized that even during seasons when I felt my life was out of control, I only had to let go and trust that God would always be there to guide me through. When I lose my nerve and begin to doubt his care, I close my eyes in prayer and hear these words just as clearly as Mia heard them when she was finally rescued: "I've got you. You're going to be just fine."

## JULY 2008

There will be times in life when we are waiting desperately for God to resolve that one thing that has been churning violently in our spirit. The wait is agony, and there is a deep, abiding fear that the answer to our request may be one we dread.

In 2008, four years before Mannard died, I felt our family heading into a tailspin when I received a call from my mother.

Mom was on the other end of the line, speaking in a faint, whispery voice—so unusual for her that it frightened me. "I'm in ER, have to have emergency surgery."

Surgery? Emergency? I had just seen her the day before at her townhouse. She was fine—a bit drawn, not her usual jovial self—but like me she was likely tired from helping prepare for our Easter dinner.

I couldn't think straight and went into a litany of questions. "Mom, what? Surgery? What's wrong with you? How did you get to the doctor? Who's there with you now?"

Mom was freakishly calm, but there was still worry in her voice. "It's blocked bowels, probably from thickened scar tissue I had from a hysterectomy a while ago, so the docs say. But I'm going to be fine—"

"I'm on my way." I rushed her off the phone and ran for my purse, texted Mannard who was at work, and told my boss I had to leave early, then raced for my car.

When I saw my mother hooked up to tubes and an IV and looking pale, I was beside myself.

"I'm still in the land of the living," Mom said with a half smile.

I sat alongside her on the bed and kissed her cheek, and our hands locked. "Yes, you are. Thank God."

She swiveled, took a good look at me, and said, "What's wrong with your hair?" She reached out to put in place the errant strands of hair I'd pulled into a sloppy bun. I stiffened and forced myself not to brush away her hand—a move I'd done since middle school when my mother went into "fix my ungroomed daughter" mode.

"What's next? When can I speak with the doctors?" I knew Mom could not be on her own just yet, and I had to create a plan of taking care of an ill parent.

"They are going to release me tomorrow. Once I get these bowels going and I walk around a bit."

"Tomorrow—that soon?" There was a lot I needed to do, such as purchase groceries, get the house in order, and prepare my kids to sleep in bunk beds in David's room. And who would care for my mother when both Mannard and I were at work?

"Yes, tomorrow." She grimaced. "The hospital needs the bed, child. No more wait until you recover well enough. They kick you out and make you fend for yourself at home."

I was over my head with worry before I left the hospital that evening, even though I assured my mother that everything would be okay.

At my house, the kids were cool with their granny coming to stay for a while. David, twelve, and Danielle, eleven, had a surefire audience since my mom played checkers and watched with enjoyment as her grandkids played video games.

Mannard pitched in and seemed not to mind having his recuperating mother-in-law in the fold. Thankfully, my husband and my mom liked and loved each other.

"Just because you're sick, Bernice, doesn't mean I'm gonna be easy on you," he said, cupping his playing cards conspiratorially during a game of spades at the kitchen table. He smacked down an ace of clubs.

Mom looked at the card and grinned. "And just because I'm not 100 percent myself doesn't mean I'm going easy on ya either, son." She thumped down an ace of spades, trumping his club.

"Oh, you're not that sick, missy," he said as he shook his head in surprise at getting beaten.

"I'm just strong," she said, pointing at her head.

Mannard nodded, and they both grinned as he shuffled the cards for another game.

Along with being my mom's entertainment, Mannard was also the heavy. Each day he would wrap his arm around her waist, holding her firm while she leaned on the banister railing, slowly laboring the fifteen stairs from the bedrooms to the lower level, tickling her with his jokes about the infirm making the mundane enjoyable. Only he could get her to walk around the house with a smile. When I tried, she gave me grumpy stares and told me to let her rest.

"Mannard has a way of making people feel good about themselves," she said as I changed the sheets on her bed one morning.

"Yes, he does. 'Cause he's so perfect," I said dryly.

In the rocker, she just watched as I slaved. "No, it's because he knows I may not be here long, so he cherishes every moment."

"Mom, the doctors said you're going to be just fine." I sighed, feeling underappreciated. "And of course Mannard is glad you're here—we all are."

"No, Mannard *wants* me here. You . . . you just tolerate me."

I felt like I had been slapped. "That's not true," I said, avoiding her eyes before taking the soiled sheets to the laundry room.

I had arranged with my boss to temporarily reduce some of my duties so my fifty- to sixty-hour-a-week job was a manageable forty hours to make sure all was well on the home front with my mom on board. Still, even with Mannard and the kids satisfied with the new arrangements, the bulk of the work was solely on me. My mother, who had been quite accommodating at the hospital when the nurses and medical staff attended to her, was not giving her daughter the same break.

"Ugh, eggs, turkey sausage, toast—again? Where's the fruit? You have any applesauce or something?" she said when I brought a tray to Danielle's room, her makeshift rehabilitation area. "Instead of all this dairy and meat, I prefer Raisin Bran or oatmeal."

"Hmm, okay, I'll get you some cereal." I trudged off to the hallway where Mannard was exiting his office, overhearing it all.

"Can you believe her?" I whispered as I followed Mannard into our bedroom, waiting to get his sympathy.

"She's used to living by herself, you know," Mannard said while sitting on the edge of the bed, putting on socks. "She likes it her way. And you probably should have asked her what types of meals she likes. They give nice, healthy options at the hospital."

I tried not to roll my eyes at him. "I didn't know I was running Detroit General."

"I'm just saying that you gotta think about how you would feel. It's tough when you're a self-sufficient person, then you take sick and are forced to rely on others."

I placed my blazer over my shoulder and grabbed my attaché case. "I still think I would be a better patient." I forced a smirk. "Not nearly as bossy."

Mannard's laugh ricocheted through the room. "You think so, huh? Well, let's hope we never find out."

* * *

My mom had been with us nearly three days when Mannard called me at work in a panic. "I came home early and your mom is in bed with a high fever. She's very lethargic."

"She was fine this morning," I said as I mentally recounted her eating oat bran and then being snug in bed before I left that morning for work.

"Yeah, I know. I'm taking her to emergency. Meet me there."

When I arrived, we got news that I had not suspected. "It's septic shock," the doctor said. "It's an infection she likely acquired here at the hospital before she left. It's serious, life-threatening . . . We're keeping her."

For five days while she was at the hospital, the staff gave her doses of antibiotics and kept a watchful eye. Mom was conscious, but it was clear that nothing was certain. In a matter of days, hours, seconds, one can be on the rebound, mending, and then go into decline. Mom could not hasten the recovery or make a deal with God to be assured everything would work in her favor.

I reached out to the Dare Divas, and they and my CTab church family prayed for Mom. Our family felt engulfed in love and care. While everyone was praying for us, we were praying for ourselves too. We felt vulnerable and yet assured at the same time that God would carry us through.

On day six, Mom was released, but this time she went to a rehabilitation facility that had expertise in elder surgery care.

While we waited on her health restoration (to God be the glory that she recovered and got back to her spitfire self ), I admittedly waited for my life to go back to normal as well. It was challenging being a caregiver, and at times very frightening. Even with the blessed rehab facility that eased my chores for my mother, I daily went by to make sure she was fed well and exercised, and I did a load of her laundry at home while doing my best to keep her spirits up.

Just as our family has had to wait on the Lord, you too will find yourself in situations in which you will have to wait. Whether you are looking to be healed, are in need of a financial breakthrough, long for the ease of your soul following the death of a loved one, or desire a wayward child to find a steely path or for a dream to come to fulfillment, it requires you to wait . . . and pray faithfully with expectation while you do so.

Seeking solace from the Bible has been instrumental in putting my life into perspective. Because here's the truth: our family and friends will not always share their personal hardships, trials, and worries; they mostly keep their troubles to themselves. And as you go through your own trials, often you will feel alone, that no one will understand. But the Bible shows examples of those who faced a storm and endured. There were times of struggle because they were human. Grief was wearisome, and they wondered why the Lord was taking so long to come to their aid.

There's Job, who had lost his children, his health, and his wealth. He was in deepest sorrow before God restored and resurrected his life with love and fulfillment.

There are other stories too: Joseph was sold into slavery by his brothers and later imprisoned, yearning for his freedom;

Abraham and Sarah waited for a child; Noah and his sons worked tirelessly for decades as they built the ark, believing the work would not be in vain.

When God has me waiting, I've come to know that he is working on me as I wait.

When my mother was ill, I had to lean into empathy and realize that it was my time to serve her. It was also a time for Mannard, the kids, and me to see ourselves as a team that worked as a unit during a crisis. It was a time for me to balance my career with what really mattered—tending to my family in need. There were so many lessons that I learned about myself and that God revealed to me. Those revelations would never have occurred until the Lord put Mom and then me into the fire so he could meld us into something new.

# 4

# dare to risk

dirt bikes, popping wheelies, and riding strong

When I was eight, Ohio Hill was the place to be. A group of little African American kids, tired of playing b-ball or climbing trees, would congregate there when our parents were busy working jobs as plant shift workers, cooks, or house cleaners—sometimes two or three jobs at a time to make ends meet.

On Ohio Hill, which was more of a large mound than a proper hill, someone had manufactured a makeshift ramp with plywood that we would launch our bicycles off of, doing tricks midair. I thought of myself as Evel Knievel, the renowned motorcycle stunt rider who launched his motorbike over buses and across canyons, when I pedaled with all my might off that thing.

Usually I played it safe, but as I watched the older boys somersault their bikes off the ramp, I knew I wanted to try it. I had just received a pink bicycle for my birthday. I was so proud when I brought it to the hill to test it out.

"You can't get the wind with this prissy thing," Brian, a kid from the neighborhood, said, batting at the sparkly tassels dangling from the handlebars.

"Yes I can!" I said as I mounted my bike in the staging area, my dark espresso skin shining from sweat. I paused a moment before I pedaled with all my might, faster than I ever had. I needed to prove myself to the other kids, and I wanted to show off what my bike could do. I launched off the ramp and soared through the air. The breeze tickled my nostrils.

But as I attempted to land, something went wrong. When my front tire touched down, I flew forward over the handlebars and landed on the packed soil.

Some of the boys laughed. I was humiliated. As I bled from both knees, I thought, *I'm not as good as them. I'm not as fast or strong. I can't do it.*

Brian shook his head and pedaled off with a few of his crew. That would be one of the first times I learned that trying new things, risky things, could wound me.

After that experience, I became a little less adventurous and a little more careful. Over time, I forgot about the exhilaration of believing I could do anything. Life experiences told me that some things just weren't worth the risk.

Childhood trauma stops many of us from moving forward or living the life we want. I look back at my younger self and wish I could encourage and steer that child into a place of bravery and confidence. Thankfully, as a mature adult, I now give myself the high fives I may need. Sometimes we just have to encourage ourselves.

• • •

More than thirty years later, I was still a pro at playing it safe. One day we visited Mannard's parents' house for Sunday dinner. Mannard patted the leather seat of his stepfather's Harley in admiration. Suited up in his leather vest that sported the logo of his biker club—the Detroit Rollers—Percy looked younger than his seventy years.

"My time is coming when I'll have my own," Mannard said, his eyes fixed on the Harley.

Percy smiled and shook his head. He was well aware of our ongoing debate about Mannard owning a bike, an argument I had always won in the past. I knew my husband to be a reasonable, smart man. But at forty-eight, him wanting to ride a motorcycle was crazy, in my opinion. We knew of more than one person who had been seriously hurt in a crash.

"Riding a motorcycle isn't inherently more dangerous than driving a car," Mannard argued now. "Actually, driver error is more likely in a car than on a bike."

Who was he kidding? I smirked and walked away, not wanting to start an argument in front of Percy.

When Mannard had first proposed the idea of getting a bike, I didn't tell him I secretly thought that riding motorcycles sounded cool—like rock-star cool. It brought to mind images of Knievel with his stunning leather jumpsuits and high-voltage smile, rocketing over buses.

Secretly, I could envision myself on a Harley or a Ducati, riding down a winding road with my hair blowing in the wind. Riding a motorcycle was delightful in my imagination; I just wasn't interested in doing it in real life—or subjecting one of my family members to such peril.

When Mannard told me about his own childhood—riding dirt bikes through his neighborhood, all Afro and skinny legs, zooming through subdivisions with friends—I tried not to smile. The joy he'd felt riding as a kid was alive and well in his heart. The longing hadn't gone away. Instead of a dirt bike, he wanted the grown-up version—a sleek Harley Davidson or a BMW.

One weekend afternoon, Mannard was watching yet another show about motorcycles as I folded laundry on the sofa beside him.

"Nope and nope," I said. "Are you trying to make me a young widow?"

Mannard attempted to charm me, batting his long eyelashes. "We can learn together, you and me," he said, taking my hand. "Community colleges offer classes, and we can get my mom and yours to watch the kids . . ."

"No," I said firmly. "Absolutely not. Why would I want to put us *both* in jeopardy?"

Mannard muted the TV and turned to me in frustration. "Then when? When will you feel okay about it? Percy is seventy! I'll bet even when I'm seventy, you'll say, 'Mannard, you're too old! Why now?'" he said in a whiny, annoying voice.

When I look back on my relationship with Mannard, I think I always had a fear of losing him. I felt that I was protecting him from himself, but deep inside I knew the one I was really trying to protect was myself. I just couldn't take the risk. I couldn't stomach the thought of anything—especially something as trivial as a motorcycle ride—ending it all.

If Mannard got a motorcycle and the worst happened, I knew that in time I could learn the mechanics of day-to-day activities and managing our finances. But in other ways, my husband was irreplaceable. I could never be a father. Both Mannard and I had missed out on the loving guidance from our own biological fathers that Mannard bestowed on David and Danielle. Whether teaching our son how to deal with bullies with integrity or showing our daughter that she was deserving of love and respect from the boys she dated, Mannard was an irreplaceable force in our family. There was a lot at stake in allowing him to pursue something so risky. I was dodging giving Mannard my okay because I feared for his life.

Finally, Mannard and I had a heart-to-heart. His desire to own a bike had not dampened; instead, it had increased. He wasn't a child and he didn't need my permission. Though he was considerate of my feelings, he finally made his decision clear as we had our weekly Wednesday night walk.

"Babe, this fear you have is real, I know," he said gently though authoritatively. "But I'm getting a bike."

The tone of his voice and his direct eye contact were such that I knew not to argue or debate. He was serious.

I thought silence would make the issue go away, but Mannard was insistent.

"The kids are in high school, so no fear of me getting hit and leaving you a widow with small children," he said, jostling my shoulder.

I didn't smile like I usually did; it wasn't funny. I just kept walking, my eyes searching his face for why he had this need for speed.

A mile into our walk I still had not responded, but it was clear that he was going to get a bike whether I was on board or not. Why make this a power play where I would whine and cause him not to share a part of his life that would bring him joy? Did I want my husband to grudgingly choose not to ride, or worse, to argue with me each time he wanted to enjoy himself?

I turned to him, and though my heart was thumping hard, I said with conviction, "Do it, Mannard. Go get your bike."

So he took a motorcycle class and passed, and within weeks he acquired a used 2003 BMW. One of the first people he visited was his stepfather to show it off.

"It's quite a bike," Percy said. "We have to ride out some-time. You know, your mother used to ride with me a lot," he said, smiling my way as I admired the bright red sheen of the motorcycle.

Mannard was shining the bike with a cloth, his pride show-ing. "Got to get Sheri on it first, and maybe some lessons."

I laughed. "You have to get in some serious mileage be-fore I get on that thing with you." I had driven my car over to meet him for dinner at the in-laws' and still wasn't too fond of the idea of him riding. Yet there was no way to discount his wide smile each time he rolled up after finish-ing a ride.

"I'll get ya." Mannard winked. "One day . . . Watch."

I rolled my eyes at such a thought. One rider in the family was plenty.

●  ●  ●

A good year after that conversation at my in-laws' house, the Divas and I met at church to put together welcome pack-ets for the outreach and development ministry.

"I think our next dare should be something cool," Mia said. "Something out there that's blow-your-mind crazy!"

"Roller coaster? Learning to swim? Hang gliding?" Brenda offered.

"Nope," Mia said. "Too tame."

Angenette rolled her eyes and shook her head in disbelief.

I glanced at Brenda with a raised eyebrow. What did those girls want? To BASE-jump off of Mount Rushmore?

Suddenly my conversation with Mannard popped into my mind. Before I could stop them, the words poured out of my mouth. "Y'all won't believe what Mannard is thinking. He wants me to learn to ride a motorcycle. Like I would ever be okay with that!"

I waited to get an "amen," but my plan backfired.

Mia's eyes popped open like I had just found the cure to cancer. "Yes! We should do it as a dare! I can see it now. First we get our motorcycle licenses. Then we get custom-made leather jackets."

"That would be so cool!" Brenda said, feeding off Mia's excitement. "With 'Dare Divas' stitched in large letters on the back."

Angenette looked at me wearily. "You've really done it now."

My eyes begged her to rescue me and halt this unruly conversation.

"It was just a joke," I said, trying to backpedal. But it was too late. The can of worms had been opened and they were never going back in.

"And the stitching can have red, pink, and purple crystals!" Mia said, her mind clearly spinning. "We would be so fly, right? I could see us riding up in the church parking lot with our jackets. Ooh-wee, won't heads turn?" She was practically shouting now. Brenda bobbed her head in agreement, and Ang smiled like the Detroit Pistons had just scored the winning shot at the buzzer.

I had hoped when I presented the Divas' idea to Mannard, he would visualize the potential catastrophe of us girls crashing into each other on the motorcycles. Instead, his response was enthusiastic. "You should absolutely do it," he said with a wide grin.

What had I just done? As Mannard turned toward his home office, I could see a bit of a swagger in his step. He thought he had won!

From that time forward, the Divas and I began plotting exactly how to execute our goal of becoming the most bedazzled biker gang in the greater Detroit area. In September 2010, we enrolled in the Schoolcraft Community College Motorcycle Safety Program. Friday night would be an in-class training, then we would embark on two full days of on-the-field instruction, learning basic skills like starting the bike, braking, shifting, maneuvering, and making turns.

Two weeks before the dare was to commence, Mia requested a teleconference. We all knew it must be urgent.

"Hey, sorry to alarm you guys," Mia said once we were on the call, "but my family is on pins and needles."

"What happened?" Brenda asked.

"My sister-in-law was just in a major motorcycle accident. She crashed into the neighbor's house, broke her wrist, and had forty stitches in her leg due to burns from the motorcycle."

"Oh, wow!" Angenette said, her deep voice hiking up a whole two octaves. "She's going to be okay, though, right?"

"She'll be fine," Mia said, "but with everything going on, I'm too shaken to bike. And I fear my family will tar and feather me if I go anywhere near a motorcycle right now. It's just not going to happen for me."

I was sorry to hear Mia's bad news, but I was also a little relieved. Could this mean the dare was off? Perhaps Jesus had sent me a divine escape. If we canceled now due to this accident, I could save face with Mannard.

"I completely understand, Mia," I spoke up. "Maybe we should just call it off, or at least delay the dare until later." I waited for the other Divas to agree with my sage wisdom.

"Divas, I also need to bow out," Angenette said. "Work is piling up with my new job, and I really need this weekend to get it together."

We paused, trying to decide what to do.

Brenda spoke first. "Mia, sis, I'm so sorry to hear about your sister-in-law. You know we all will be sending our prayers, and you shouldn't ride if you're not feeling good about it."

I waited for Brenda to throw the conciliatory white flag on the dare.

"I'll be praying for you both," she continued. "But, Sheri, I don't see a need to cancel. I borrowed a helmet and have my boots and gloves. I'm ready. So I'll see you at class next Friday. I'm looking forward to it."

Brenda was going to follow through on our plans, which meant I had no excuse not to join her. "I'll be there," I said much more cheerfully than I felt.

As I hung up the phone in the kitchen, Mannard was standing nearby, making a tuna sandwich.

"Ugghhh." I grimaced, shaking my fist in the air.

"Motorcycle dare still happening?" Mannard said, a stupid grin on his face.

I couldn't help it. I swatted him on the backside with a towel a little harder than I'd planned.

"Ouch!" he cried out. "What did I do?"

I looked at my conniving hubby trying to appear innocent.

"You know what you did!" I tried not to laugh as I went upstairs. How had I gotten myself roped into this outlandish dare?

At the Friday night class, our instructor played instructional videos that explained the mechanics of the motorcycle and provided simulations. We learned about what was permitted and prohibited under Michigan law when riding. Around forty of us received a briefing on motorcycle safety, what to do in an emergency, and how to obey traffic laws. The rules made me feel better about this whole endeavor. I left that night feeling a little less daunted by the challenges ahead. Maybe I wouldn't die in this class after all.

Before a highly unskilled person such as myself was given control over this powerful machine, I would receive sufficient instruction and preparation. I would not be thrown into a dangerous, unknown situation.

This reminds me of how God gives us teachings in his manual, the Bible. He also places people in our lives whom we can trust to instruct us.

● ● ●

The next morning, the first day of the practical instruction for my motorcycle class, Mannard walked me out to the car. "Go get 'em," he said, placing a bright red helmet on my head and securing the strap. He had chosen the helmet and purchased it for me as a gift. "Dang, you look good!"

"I don't want to go," I said. "This is your fault. If you hadn't started all of this, I wouldn't be risking life and limb right now!"

Mannard tried to hide his smile. "Now, now! I'm so proud of you. I may come and watch."

"Come on, then!" I said, unsnapping the helmet and removing it. "I could use the extra support. It's not too late."

"Nope. It's a Diva dare. You'll be fine. Now GO!" He pushed me gently into the driver's seat. "Whoop whoop! Go girl! Go girl!" he chanted.

Sometimes I just couldn't stand my husband. He was so cute and annoying at the same time.

When I arrived at the class, I saw forty-five Kawasaki motorcycles grouped into sets of eight throughout Schoolcraft's parking lot. The bikes looked worn—like they'd been driven around the equator.

"These bikes are sturdy and safe, time tested," our instructor, Bill, assured us. He had long white hair and a flowing beard to match. "Now grab a bike," he instructed our group of six. "Any one you fancy."

I picked a solid gray one. In addition to the bike looking ancient, it was covered in dust that transferred to my backside. My jeans took on a chalky blue sheen.

There were forty of us total in the group, half of us female. Each smaller group of six to eight had its own mini course with orange cones and white directional lines on black asphalt. We practiced clutch and throttle coordination as we walked our bikes with the motor running. This allowed us to get comfortable with the bikes before driving them.

Bill explained that our main goal for the two days was to

stay atop our bikes. Falling off or having our bikes slip to the ground would result in an immediate fail and dismissal from class.

As Bill was reviewing the overall mechanics of the bike from the videos the night before, Brenda whispered, "What is that acronym? The one from class that the instructor said we'd need to know today—'SEE'? I can't remember."

"Search. Evaluate. Execute," I said. I'd spent a good two hours the night before committing my notes to memory.

Bill explained that we would be learning to perform a series of skills: weaving between cones, turning corners, making U-turns, shifting gears, accelerating, slowing, stopping, and avoiding hazards by braking and swerving.

"My goal is to make sure you know what you're doing when you leave this class," Bill said, "so you don't injure or kill yourself or anyone else. No injuries. No fatalities. If I feel in any way that you don't quite have it or if you need some more hours of training, you will *not* get your certificate this weekend. If that's the case, no worries. You'll get there with more training hours."

While Brenda and I both wanted that piece of paper, mounting those motorcycles was the dare. Earning a license would be a bonus.

"Now say it with me," Bill said.

"No injuries. No fatalities," we repeated in unison.

As I mounted my bike, I said a silent prayer for no injuries that weekend. I started the engine and let it idle as Bill went from student to student, helping us get comfortable with the bikes beneath us.

Brenda looked like a certified biker chick with her leather boots, jeans, helmet, and gloves. When it was her turn, she

86

masterfully took the bike up to forty-five miles per hour and halted within inches of the orange cone.

I wasn't as successful. When it was my turn, I ambled my way up to speed, but when it was time to stop, I didn't just topple my cone; I smashed it into the ground.

"Next time, Hunter," Bill said, motioning to the next rider to take their position.

I looked over at Brenda, who shrugged her shoulders in an "oh well, you're doing fine" gesture.

As the day went on, my confidence grew. It was a sunny, eighty-five-degree day, and I was dressed in boots, jeans, and a long jacket. Even though I was sweating profusely, I could not deny that I was actually *enjoying* the dare (gasp!).

Brenda was feeling the same, judging by her big, beautiful smile. She was performing quite well. We exchanged a high five after we both easily wove through a series of cones. Most importantly, with half the day gone, neither of us had dropped our bikes.

"Girl, I see us in those leather jackets already," Brenda said.

I was glad to see her confidence, but we still had another full day ahead. "Yep, we are on our way," I said, wrapping my hands over her shoulders. "Ang and Mia are gonna be so jealous when they see the pics of all the fun we're having."

Brenda snorted. "Yeah, let's tell them that it was all fun and games," she said. Sweat dripped from beneath her helmet down her forehead. "But we know the real deal."

• • •

When I returned home at the end of the day, Mannard was waiting for me in the driveway. He was lathering up the car, waiting to hear of the day's events.

"Well, you're not banged up," he said as I brushed past him. I wanted to get into a nice warm shower and get the musk from the day off me.

He followed behind, leaving the half-washed car. "Sooo, how was it?" He waited eagerly, his teeth clenched. I knew he was hoping that I hadn't failed the first day—or decided to bail, realizing I really was a spa girl instead of a Hells Angel.

"I'm filthy, my hair is matted from sweating underneath that helmet, and I smell like gasoline." I paused for effect, not wanting to own what was a surprise to myself. "And I loved it." I sighed. "Every stinky, exhausting moment of it."

Mannard jumped and pumped his fist in the air. "I knew it! When you didn't call home in a panic or ask me to come pick you up, I knew you were on your way to becoming a biker chick," he said with a wink.

"Not so fast. I'm not about to saddle up on a bike anytime soon. This is just a dare." I paused before saying, "But I do see why you like . . . why you wanted to have your own motorcycle."

●  ●  ●

The next day of class proved that the first day had just been a warm-up. The skill required went up dramatically. We had to ride our bikes in a figure eight, in a tight enough radius that I had to lean with the bulk of my weight shifted to one hip, ride the clutch, and turn, all while balancing the bike. If I tilted it too much I could lose control and spill the bike.

We watched two riders attempt to maneuver through the course and lose their balance. They both fell to the ground along with their bikes, which resulted in immediate failure of the course. Bill said if this happened to us, we were welcome to stick around, but the first two people who dropped their bikes left immediately—I imagined from embarrassment.

"I think the trick is to angle your knee outward as you lean and lift off the clutch a bit," Brenda said as she studied the next rider. "See, she's going to make it. She has her body weighted just right."

Brenda was correct. The rider, who appeared to be no more than a hundred pounds, mastered the machine beneath her. She completed the figure eight with a round of applause for being the first to do so. I was up next.

"Sheri, if you feel the bike is getting away from you, don't worry about completion," Brenda coached. I listened since she was a natural, one of the stars of the class. "Remember, there's a total number of points needed. If you don't complete this one you can still get your license. Just don't fall."

She was right. The problem was, every point mattered. I hadn't been doing as well as Brenda, and I was beginning to doubt I would be able to earn enough points to pass. Moments earlier, I had dodged running into another rider. Overall, my riding afforded lots of room for improvement.

After Brenda's coaching, I mounted my bike and waited for the instructor's signal to begin.

I felt comfortable on the bike as I saddled up, though a bit nervous with all eyes on me. I eased into the bottom half of the figure eight, using my pedal to clutch. Ever so slowly, I completed the first oval as I made my way to complete the second one. But I was moving a bit too slowly and could feel the bike beginning to tip. I revved my engine, attempting to keep the bike upright. As I did, the bike lurched to the right, taking me off the edge of the white spray-painted line on the asphalt. I would not get the fifteen points, as the figure eight was beyond my skill level. But I didn't fall.

Brenda was next. I watched my friend from a few feet away. Her face was set in fierce determination as she jostled the bike, willing it to come under her command. I wished that her husband and kids could have seen her like this. She completed the exercise with precision, and the edge of her tire stayed on the white line. I was so proud of her.

But by the end of the day, neither of us had completed all the exercises with the skill needed to earn our certificate. A little off speed here, a shaky turn there, or a miscalculation with our timing shaved just enough off our total. Our points simply didn't add up.

"Listen," Bill said, "most people have to take this class twice. Most of the people who earned their license today are taking their second or third class. Sign up again and try to get it next time."

I didn't feel like I deserved a certificate, but I felt like Brenda had been robbed.

"I think they fail folks intentionally to make sure people take the class at least twice!" she said as we headed back to our cars. I was sure the true reason was safety, but I was still miffed that my friend hadn't passed.

"I thought you did really well, Brenda," I said.

Mannard had once told me that I am a conspiracy theorist with a distrust of institutions. A part of me wanted to confront the instructor and challenge his decision on my friend's behalf. But, like in many cases before—at church, as a leader of the contact outreach ministry, and even with the Dare Divas—Brenda was a better sport than me.

She shrugged. "I could have done better," she said. "It probably is a good idea to take another class. I saw a driver almost hit a biker on my way to class this morning. To be honest, I wouldn't feel comfortable being on the road yet—for myself or others."

When I arrived home, I told Mannard, "I didn't pass." I handed over my helmet to him with a disappointed smile. "Didn't drop the bike, but didn't get that license either."

He pulled me to him and whispered in my ear, "You're my Wonder Woman, babe. Always."

And he was my Superman. I felt a smile form on my lips as I pulled him into a sweaty hug.

• • •

The following spring in May, Mannard convinced me to retake the class with him. This time I did it willingly.

The second day of our class, Mannard gunned the engine too forcefully and dropped the bike. Immediate fail—and he had already passed a previous class and was a safe motorcyclist. We chalked it up to it being a bad bike (wink).

"How did that happen?" he said. He seemed taken aback. "Man, I'm on the road now. I'm going to take another class. That kind of stuff can't happen on the road."

I wrapped my arm around his broad shoulders. "We're in this together, babe. Next time." I didn't pass either. We retook the class, and that time we both passed, and I had my own license and certification.

On our first ride, three weeks after we'd passed the class, I wrapped my arms tightly around Mannard's waist. The wind made my eyes water as Mannard drove us out of our neighborhood. I was confident riding behind him on the seat. Investing in the classes had paid off.

"You okay back there?" he asked at a stoplight.

"I'm doing great." I smiled and pressed my cheek to the back of his jacket. "Never been better."

Mannard had purchased a red, white, and black leather jacket and his own red helmet to match his shiny red BMW. He looked so handsome and was the talk of the neighborhood. I smile now, thinking of the pleasure and great enjoyment he got out of that used motorcycle.

Learning to ride motorcycles drew Mannard and me closer together. It wasn't my initial desire, but us being on bikes together put a sparkle in my man's eyes. I don't regret that one bit.

• • •

One morning Mannard rode his motorcycle to church while I drove the kids. The guys at church were impressed at Mannard's skill. They were even more impressed that he had convinced me to allow him to get a bike.

One woman whose kids were younger than mine approached me in awe. "George wants to get a bike," she said, "and seeing Mannard on his made him even more excited. I'm just so nervous. Aren't you? I can't imagine what I'd do if anything happened to him."

I held her hand and smiled, recalling the promise Mannard had made, that he wouldn't purchase a bike until the kids were older.

"I get it, sis," I told her. "But every time Mannard talks about the bike, comes back from riding it, or even just works on it, it gives him so much joy. I had to give in. I surrendered to it."

Mannard rode that bike for two years before he died. And despite all my fear surrounding him riding a bike, it wasn't a motorcycle crash that took him from me. It was his heart. No amount of caution could have prevented what happened that morning in August.

I am so thankful that I honored and supported Mannard's dream, even though it took me a while to get there. If he had not had the opportunity to own that motorcycle, I would have always looked back with sadness that he didn't get a chance to do what he dreamed of—to relive the freedom of his childhood, the wind blowing on his face.

A few years after Mannard's death, I saw George again on his own bike in the church parking lot. I gave him a high five.

He smiled with a hint of sadness in his eyes. "I saw Mannard do it, and I had to do it too." He hugged me, and we both beamed.

"You've got to live, right?" I said. "We've all gotta live and enjoy what we can, while we can, for as long as we can." I said the words to encourage him, but I hoped they would become my mantra.

Mannard's shiny red motorcycle sat in the garage for months after he died. I didn't know what to do with it. Should I sell it? Give it away? I didn't really want to keep it. The bike was a bit too tall for me to ride (Mannard was six feet; I was five four), and I had never driven a bike on the open road, just on the Schoolcraft course.

I visited the dealership where Mannard had purchased the bike to see if they would sell it for me.

"You sure you don't want to keep it or ride it one last time?" the salesman asked. "We can lower the chassis."

I allowed them to custom-fit the bike, Mannard's bike,

to my smaller frame and took it home again. Some days I'd hop on it and just sit, thinking that one day I might ride it. Some days I'd wipe it down with a dry cloth, as Mannard had often done. I didn't know if I'd ever have the courage to ride it—to zoom down Woodward Avenue as Mannard had on many fine evenings and each Sunday after church.

I did ride the bike once more. It was wiggly at first as the wheel skirted down our drive, and then I took one final loop around our block. That's as long a ride as I could muster confidently—a triumph ride . . . for Mannard.

Had I known that my beloved would be gone so soon, I certainly would have championed him getting that motorcycle sooner. *Had I known.* His dream had been delayed. And while I was thankful that he had those two precious years to do what he had longed to do since his youth, I'd often wonder how much more enjoyment—how many more years he could have had—if I hadn't held him back.

Through getting my motorcycle license, I learned that some risks are worth taking. When I first agreed to the dare, I did it because I was a Dare Diva. I wanted to unite in solidarity with my friends and earn those sparkly leather jackets. But I later realized there was another reason I did it: I wanted my husband to know he married someone exciting, interesting, and brave.

When I fell off my bike as a little girl after attempting to soar, a part of me didn't want to take a chance again. I wanted full assurance that everything would work out just right before I took another risk. I didn't want to go for it again only to have my heart broken. And that fear masquerading as good sense followed me throughout my life.

This time was different. I had mounted that motorcycle repeatedly. Twice I failed and chose to try again. Three times

I sat through hours of instruction to learn a new skill. Three times I did something unfamiliar and difficult. And with each try I gained confidence that I didn't have before. The Lord was showing me that I could be filled with anticipation without assurances. He was restoring my belief that I could fly like Evel Knievel. It would take time. In fact, it might take much more time than I expected, but I should never lose my zeal for living. The doing, the living, the risking through Christ, is what makes it all worthwhile.

# 5

# dare to be bold

### even the Eiffel Tower is not too tall for a Diva

**JANUARY 2014**

"Dare-apy" was changing me at my core. In the seventeen months since Mannard's passing, God had been setting me up to think and traverse well outside my comfort level. The change began with the dares. The Divas and I had gone whitewater rafting, cliff jumping, skiing, motorcycling, and winter zip-lining. At first, each of those dares had seemed impossible and beyond my skills and ability, but I had overcome and I had loved every one!

As I pushed myself physically to do things I never would have imagined doing, my courage began to extend to other areas of my life. The "extreme" challenges at home, from giving away my husband's clothes and organizing my finances to raising my children as a single mom, became something to conquer with God's supernatural strength. And in the

97

months since my husband's untimely death, God had faithfully helped me overcome each challenge that came my way. I could feel my boldness growing. I was ready to do whatever God was calling me to. The thing was, I had no idea what that calling was. What was the next big thing in my life?

No one could answer that but me. Mannard wasn't there to encourage and push me to step out. The Dare Divas gave me high fives but couldn't assure me that I was not making a hideous mistake. Same with my mom and kids. They wanted me to be happy, but no one could confirm what was the best thing for me.

I listened to sermons, including those of my pastor, Dr. James Morman, in an effort to gain some perspective. I kept hearing the same thing: I would know if a new, open door—an opportunity—was from God. And if the path I chose was from God, it would not contradict his Word. There would be confirmation along the way, and it would require me to rely on him.

Now I encourage everyone to find out what tools and resources bring out the best in them, and to have a Scripture or nugget of wisdom as a personal mantra. Memorizing Scripture and applying it to those times when I needed direction brought me a lot of peace.

* * *

About a week before my husband died, I sat across the table from him at our favorite soul food bistro and looked at him. Still handsome, although his curly Afro was gone. It had been replaced long ago by whispers of hair along the perimeter of his head. I didn't tell him he needed a haircut. And I knew he didn't mind my less-than-stylish messy bun one little bit. We were in our own rhythm of perfect contentedness.

I had no idea that one week later that comfortable life would be no more—our steady rhythm would be replaced by the unimaginable. During those first few weeks, I stumbled through the motions of life, feeling numb. I missed the little things: sharing a good meal with him or snuggling up next to him at the end of a long day. He was better than any blanket. I didn't miss the big, romantic gestures as much as the ordinary, everyday routine we had established together.

Even a year and a half after his death, many days were filled with reminders of him. As my grief progressed, I began to feel an itch to get away. So many things in my life reminded me of Mannard, and I craved a change of scenery.

One morning as I was having breakfast with the Divas at our favorite pancake house in Detroit, I told them about my idea to take a round-the-world cruise out of South Africa.

Brenda took a bite of her omelet. "I'd rather you not go alone," she said. "What if you get sick?"

I leaned toward her and touched my cheek to hers. "I know," I said. "I wish you all could come with me, even for a little bit."

"Wait," Mia said, peeking over the brochure I'd handed her like she'd had a revelation. "Are you flying directly to Africa?"

"No," I answered. "I'll go to Paris first, then South Africa."

"Perfect!" Mia exclaimed. "Divas, what do you think about joining Sheri in Paris? Can we do that?" Her eyes had the same sparkle they'd had when she asked us to go on our first dare, whitewater rafting. "We can begin the journey with our sis! Paris for three days or so, then Sheri can fly to South Africa."

I beamed at Mia. She was brilliant!

"Like a bon voyage," Angenette said. "Let's do it!"

We intertwined our hands in the middle of the table, our bright smiles illuminating our circle.

"Dare Divas unite," Brenda said.

"Dare Divas unite!"

•   •   •

Even with the Divas committing to join me in Paris, I still doubted my decision to travel. Was I running away from my troubles instead of dealing with them? Although I was starting to feel "normal" again, sometimes the four walls of my life at home seemed to be closing in on me. With the kids in college, I lived alone in the house where Mannard had died—the brick colonial where we'd painted the walls, sent our kindergarteners off to school, and shared Thanksgiving dinners. But it had all been marred that morning Mannard died without warning.

In the year and a half since, I'd often sought solace in my cozy chair with my Bible and a cup of tea. When I needed to get out, I went to the corner java house, put on my headphones, and listened to the teachings of some of my favorite preachers. Walks helped too. Being out in nature, hearing the birds and smelling the wildflowers, comforted my aching soul.

I knew that healing did not require a transatlantic trip abroad. And yet, I sensed an open door of opportunity that might not come again. My children were healthy, my mom was well, and I had the stamina, desire, and resources to go.

Losing my husband had changed my perspective. I now knew life was short and the clock was ticking. Psalm 90:12

says, "Teach us to number our days, that we may gain a heart of wisdom." I never really understood that until I lost my vibrant husband in the prime of his life. Mannard had no idea that fifty years was all he would have. God was teaching me that I had no assurance of when my time would be up either. I knew I could wait until I was retired to take a trip like this, but I also felt a strong conviction that I needed to *live now*.

This journey would be a huge leap for me. I had legitimate fears. Was it wise to travel alone? Was I wasting precious resources that could be better spent elsewhere? Would I even achieve my goal of learning what the Lord had next for me? What if he didn't answer? These questions and others nagged at me.

Perhaps it was my newfound boldness from attempting death-defying feats, but I decided to take the leap. This trip would require that I lean on the Lord and trust him. I would have to depend on him for protection and provision. And I would have to trust that as I earnestly sought him, he would show me the right path moving forward. So I packed my bags.

* * *

I gripped the seat in front of me as our double-decker tour bus careened along the streets of Place Charles de Gaulle, ushering us through the hot spots of Paris. Our first day in the city was already proving to be quite a ride. We were on the top of the open-air bus. We shivered as the forty-degree chill froze our smiles in place.

When the bus stopped for a moment, Angenette seized her opportunity. "If we hunch our knees, we can all get in the frame with the Arc de Triomphe behind us," she said. Angenette is the selfie queen and self-appointed Diva photographer. The rest of us were less enthusiastic as the bus lurched forward again and we fought to keep our balance. Despite Ang's zeal for capturing the perfect selfie, I was having an amazing time in Paris with my three best friends.

The Divas had agreed to join me in Paris to celebrate my forty-seventh birthday before I embarked on further travel. The first time I visited Paris in September 2001, there were no selfies with girlfriends. I was happily married to Mannard, and we were celebrating our tenth wedding anniversary. We'd set off for a trip to London to visit friends. After London we traveled to Paris. I had never been to Europe before, and I didn't want to just *see* Paris, I wanted to *experience* it. Mannard and I went to the Eiffel Tower, the Louvre, and the Notre Dame cathedral, and I quickly fell in love with the beautiful city.

We visited the bookstalls that lined the Seine River, flipped through the mountain of books at Shakespeare and Company, and admired its ornate drinking fountain dating from the nineteenth century. Then there was shopping at the Marais—or, on our budget, window shopping—and strolling through boutiques and ateliers displaying the craftsmanship of Parisian designers.

For me, there was this great sense of freedom in Paris, something I had never experienced before. I could see myself living there. With Paris as my hub, I could explore other areas: Spain, England, Greece. Mannard and I could hop on the metro to the ballet at Palais Garnier or to an auction at Drouot. I could learn to cook classic dishes like *sole meunière*, pressed duck, roast chicken, bistro-style veal liver, *pâté en croûte*, onion soup, and *entrecôte*. I could learn to speak French, discuss politics, and walk our toddlers through lovely parks and gardens like Parc Monceau, Parc de Bercy, and Parc de Belleville.

"Maybe you can get a gig here for a while," I said to my sweetie. We sat eating chocolate croissants and drinking espresso while people-watching at a local café.

At the time, Mannard worked for IBM as a consultant and had been on assignment in Japan, but we had not been relocated there. I didn't mind. We had small children, and I had no fantasies of Japan at the time. But *Paris*! In Paris I could get lost, devour art and history . . . all on IBM's dime, of course.

"But I don't speak French," Mannard replied matter-of-factly. "And?"

"You know how many people at my job would give their left lung for an assignment in Paris? Fluency in French would definitely be a requirement, and I'm sure it would go to someone higher up the corporate ladder than me."

"Are you sure?"

"Look, it's not happening. Dream on, babe."

"Just check," I pleaded. "You can give up a lung."

But it wasn't to be. After the 2004 economic downturn, Mannard lost his job at IBM, and we were barely able to scrape enough savings together to pay the mortgage until another job came along nine months later. Even during that rough patch when the employment checks were coming to an end, I wasn't troubled. I was probably naive, but I knew Mannard would take care of it, that he'd make it all right. He always did. But once he passed, I had to actively push myself to no longer be that woman underneath someone's wing, looking for a man to shelter and save me. I was working on it, even though I had not yet arrived.

●  ●  ●

My second visit to Paris was very different from the first. Instead of enjoying one of the most romantic cities in the world with my love, this trip was supposed to take my mind off him. It wasn't working. I was reminded of him constantly as I reminisced about the romantic vacation we had enjoyed together all those years before.

When the Divas and I ordered and devoured chocolate croissants, I remembered the time Mannard and I had savored each buttery, decadent bite as I'd gently brushed crumbs from his lips. On our day cruise on the Seine, I remembered how I'd laid my head on Mannard's shoulder and held his strong hand.

At the Pont des Arts, we walked the bridge above the Seine and viewed hundreds of "love locks" attached to the fence, representing the many lovers who had visited. In 2001, the tradition had not yet begun. Part of me wished a lock was there for Mannard and me—tangible evidence of our time together in Paris.

Our tour bus's first stop was Notre Dame de Paris. We were awed by the cathedral's impressive French Gothic architecture with stained glass. Centuries-old bodies of bishops and cardinals resided there, and I couldn't help but think of death. *Tomb. Burial. Gone.*

My own church, Christian Tabernacle, came to mind—those years where Mannard and I served in ministry side by side and saw heaven touch earth as we watched people come to know Christ and develop deeper relationships with him. My mind was spiraling, and fresh pain washed over me. *Did*

*I make the wrong decision coming on this trip?* I thought. *Will I be sorrowful the entire time?*

"Earth to Sheri." Brenda's voice broke into my reverie.

"I'm here," I whispered. Though I was present in body, I was thinking of what could have been had Mannard still been alive.

Beneath the stone walls were the entombed. There was no need for fumigation, as their bodies were long past the ripe phase. I thought of my sweetie in his resting place and wondered how that term came to be. *Resting* would mean he was at home, breathing, sitting in his favorite chair in our den, his legs kicked up, sipping on his decaf coffee with a splash of half-and-half. Instead, his "resting place"—the crypt, the mausoleum—was doused with chemicals each night to kill gnats, those pesky, intuitive dipterans that can sniff out rotting flesh even when it's behind six feet of stone. The structure closed at 8:00 some evenings to prevent folks from gagging on the fumes.

Mia was flipping her tourist map again. "Notre Dame, done. Now we need to hightail it to the Louvre." She had a long list of everything we needed to attack before our three days in Paris were up. "If we hit the Louvre, it may take two hours," she said, her eyes focused on the map.

"No way," Brenda interrupted. "Four, at least. We can't possibly see it all in two hours."

Brenda liked to fully take in a sight before moving on. She wanted to inhale it, let it soak in, and she was perfectly okay with not visiting every must-see sight. "There's always next time," she'd say with confidence, accepting that if next time didn't come, this time was enough. I loved her childlike wonder.

"We can spend a whole week in the Louvre, but we just don't have the time," Mia said. "We can do four hours, but that means less time at Versailles. And you did say you wanted to get those chocolate croissants."

While Brenda and Mia negotiated the itinerary, Ang and I sat down on a bench, taking in the beauty around us. Two alpha females on the case was plenty. Ang was like me when it came to travel—sit back, soak it in, let it wash over you. Embrace the *right now*. That is, unless that perfect selfie was at stake—then Angenette was on a mission to document the moment for all posterity. We all had our travel quirks, but that was part of the fun.

"How are you doing?" Ang said.

"I'm okay. Still can't believe I'm doing this," I said, waving my hand across the stunning view of Parisian architecture before us. "And then the cruise." Feelings of doubt washed over me, and I could feel the tears coming.

Angenette grasped my hand. "Sis, look at all you've done, all that you've been through, since Mannard passed. I am *positive* God will not forsake you now. I know it's hard to be here without him, but God is doing a new thing, and it's good."

"Girl, it's so funny you can see what I can't. Losing Mannard has been harder than I ever imagined."

"You're packing up your house," Ang said, touching my arm. "Your life—box by box. You should pat yourself on the back."

I laughed. "It's not a choice. I wish it was. But the mortgage company would kick my behind out if I didn't."

Ang gave me a hard look. "Stop it, Sheri. You did have a choice. You found a solution to short-sell your house. Stop downplaying everything you do. Give yourself some credit! You're getting unstuck and you're moving forward!"

She raised her hand for a high five, and I smacked it with conviction. She was right. Small movement was still movement, and I was definitely moving forward.

A few minutes later, we were back on track. There was a serious rush to get to the Louvre, but my friends' true intentions were as transparent as tissue paper. Their real mission was to keep me busy so that I was focused on fun, not loss. They figured all the beauty and activity might distract me from my gloomy thoughts.

We arrived at the Louvre and went inside. A crowd had formed near the Renaissance paintings. I gazed at one of the Last Supper and another of Jesus on the cross with a criminal on either side and the Virgin Mary weeping at his feet. My throat tickled just a bit, though it was hard to say exactly why. Was it the despair I saw in a mother viewing the horrible death of her son? Perhaps it was my Christian faith bubbling inside me as I thought of my Savior's great sacrifice, or perhaps the painting hit a nerve as I thought of my own loss and grief.

As Mia and I walked along the limestone path to meet up with Brenda and Ang, I thought about how funny life was. Everything in the museum seemed so important, but one day I would leave it all behind as Mannard had done and have no further concern for the world or the honors it provided.

At the next exhibit, Mia angled her camera for the perfect shot. She and Ang seemed to be having a competition for the record of the most pictures captured in Paris in a three-day run. "Ugh, if only I can get this camera to cooperate," Mia said, straightening up to her whole five-foot-one stature. In the thick of the crowd, her elbow slightly nipped another photo enthusiast's hip, and he gave her some serious side eye. But Mia was too focused to notice his annoyance. Everyone was jockeying for position to create a memory—a perfect snapshot to prove that it really happened.

I have always been one who wants to insert myself into the moment instead of capturing it. Feeling the sun on my skin at the top of the Eiffel Tower, frolicking along the Seine, smelling the flowers at Versailles—those were the moments I had cherished with Mannard in Paris. Thankfully, they were also in a photo album, courtesy of my photo-snapping husband, who had all the enthusiasm of Mia on that trip. I realized how precious those pictures were to me. I no longer had anyone to smile at me and recall the time when the light hit the Pont Alexandre III just right and we spotted a luxurious rainbow as we crossed the bridge. I had no one with whom to share stories of how happy we'd been as we strolled through Sainte-Chapelle, the impressive gothic-style royal chapel. I turn to those images in bound scrapbooks now and commit those stories to heart, since Mannard is no longer here to reflect on them with me.

We inched farther down the corridor to view the *Mona Lisa*, said to be the most well-known painting in the world. I was struggling to understand why. The figure in front of me with the alabaster skin and dingy brown hair was so, well, *drab*. I wondered what da Vinci saw in Mona Lisa or why millions of people still find her so intriguing. She's not even cute. She's just sitting there, all docile, not a rowdy bone in her body.

Hordes of people seemed intrigued by her image, so I took a deeper look. Maybe they saw what I didn't. The Divas had wandered to other parts of the collection, so there I stood. Mona Lisa's face was brightly lit and framed with various darker elements—the veil, her hair—which made me take notice of the more subtle nuances of her face. Her eyes weren't sad, but they weren't gleeful either. And what was up with that half smile?

I imagined sitting for a portrait. I'd likely be filled with random thoughts of the thousands of things I could be doing instead of sitting with an artist—writing poetry or love letters, tending sheep, preparing delicious vittles. What exactly was there to do back in the sixteenth century during Mona's time, anyway? Maybe she'd broken it off with a lover or had just lost her husband. Maybe she wasn't that different from me after all.

After spending seven hours in the Louvre, not nearly enough time to do its massive three wings justice, we headed to the Eiffel Tower. The first order of business when we arrived was to don our Dare Diva T-shirts, the brainchild of Mia, the fashionista of our group. Still feeling down from a day packed with memories of Mannard, I wanted to get our visit over with, go back to the hotel, and pull the plush comforters over my weepy eyes. But *noooo*, we had to take the pictures—in our black *short-sleeve* T-shirts in the middle of January! Before our trip Mia had purchased the bedazzled tees as a surprise, and she'd presented them to us over breakfast earlier that day.

"Mia, you are so thoughtful. The T-shirts are so cute," I said.

"What a Diva," Angenette said, hugging hers to her chest.

"Only Mia," Brenda said, hugging Mia around the waist.

I didn't tell them about my previous visit to the Eiffel Tower with Mannard. Or that all the emotions I'd been feeling all day were overwhelming. The point was to be happy. You don't go to Paris and talk about your husband who died on a rainy morning. Paris does not do gloomy. This is the land of *ooohs* and *ahhhs*.

In order to see the beauty of the gems on these glam tees, we had to remove our jackets. The tourists around us wore down coats, wool jackets, and puffer coats. It was a blustery, cold day, and folks walking past us did a double take, because why oh why would anyone want to dress like they were summering in the Adirondacks when it was thirty-five degrees?

"That's not it," Mia said when I shared my theory. "They think we're celebrities."

"And why would they think that? This isn't a photo shoot." I held up my camera. "Got it from Costco. It's not a Nikon, and I'm not Annie Leibovitz."

"They're looking at us because we are *amazing*." Mia laughed. "Have you seen anyone else like us around?"

The three of us looked at our captain, who had clearly gone rogue.

"Too much wine," Ang said.

"And chocolate!" Brenda snorted and blew a kiss at Mia, who looked slightly offended.

Mia must have noticed the dark cloud over my face. She brushed off the teasing, came up from behind, and hugged me. "Come now, sis. Cheer up."

We took turns taking pics with each other. We clowned around, made odd faces, kicked our legs high like chorus girls, and made the peace sign, all with the Eiffel Tower in the background. Soon a small crowd of people formed around us, smiling and laughing along with us. And just like that, my melancholy subsided.

Suddenly a guy rushed up from behind us, his hands moving toward my camera. I started, wondering if he was a thief trying to snatch my camera.

He smiled broadly. "Me, uh, I take your picture?"

*Right. I'm from Detroit. That's not gonna work, you crook.*

"No, no, but thanks," I said.

Three other men joined him. They were dressed in stylish cashmere caps and tailored glen plaid overcoats. These were the most nicely dressed robbers I had ever seen. They were young, probably late twenties or early thirties, with lean physiques and bright white smiles.

"You ladies are beautiful. Where you from?" The young man looked like a movie star. I detected a possibly Croatian accent.

"Where do you think we are from?" Ang asked.

"US, I guess." He eyed our flashy attire. "Not French, I'm sure. No French accent."

"No, we are not from France." I pursed my lips and tried not to bat my eyelashes. I couldn't help but be smitten by his good looks. "We're from Detroit."

"Motown!" his friends exclaimed. "Motown! We love the music. Wow. *Fantastico!* Some of the best of music of all time."

I smiled at their appreciation of Detroit culture. There were so many things we could be proud of, hailing from Michigan. The Big Three automobile manufacturers, the Great Lakes, and, of course, the electrifying music of the Motown era.

The one with the Prada glasses and skinny jeans began to sing "Baby, I Need Your Loving." Whatever fear we had about these guys dissipated, and soon we were dancing and singing in the park with our newfound Croatian friends.

Around the park, there were no faces like ours. We saw no other chocolate or caramel or toffee faces. And if that wasn't enough to make us stand out, we were wearing our short-sleeve shirts.

"Picture with us, please?" Two young brunettes, one sporting a smart Parisian tam and the other with an "I Luv Paris" tee peeking out from her fur coat, held up their cameras. "Are you here filming?" they asked. "A documentary? A reality show?"

"Do we look like we are?" Mia asked, giving me an "I told you so" look. I nearly grabbed the first woman's tam and hurled it at Mia.

"You look like celebrities," the other woman said in an Irish accent. She was probably no older than twenty-five.

I rolled my eyes. *Really?* "We're not celebrities."

She handed me her camera anyway. "Doesn't matter. Family at home won't know."

*Exactly*, I thought. *What happens in Paris stays in Paris.*

Going on trips with the girls can be . . . girlie! It allows us to just be carefree and childlike. Have you ever thought of taking the initiative of getting together with a group of girls or just one special friend and jaunting off? If there's something holding you back, I'd suggest taking a deep breath and just packing your bags!

●  ●  ●

"So tomorrow you're off to Africa." Brenda reached for my hand, and I folded mine over hers. "How you feeling?"

"Nervous, happy, scared, excited." I shook my head and sighed at the hodgepodge of emotions. "But I am going. Too late to back out now. I'm really glad you guys came for the great sendoff."

"We're happy to be here," Brenda said. She paused. "And what you're feeling . . . I'd feel that way too." She handed me a gift bag. I reached inside to discover a book about writing and its spiritual aspects. "You are so talented, my friend," she said. "I don't think you know just how much your writing affects people."

I hugged her. "Thanks, Bren. I just sometimes get so frustrated. Nothing substantial seems to happen with it. Articles here and there, but I can't quit my day job."

"Not yet, but maybe soon. Just keep at it. Don't give up. I can see you taking your writing to another level."

That night we got dressed up and went to Moulin Rouge to celebrate my birthday. We sipped cabernet and teased each other about our many mishaps, the young Croatian men, and our mistaken identities as celebrities. We'd also had a minor mishap on the subway when we exited before our stop and found ourselves in a hair store with purple, pink, and other fluorescent-colored wigs.

"*Essaye le, essaye le* [try it, try it]! She wanted me to put that thing on!" Mia laughed hard at the memory of the store owner trying desperately to affix an apple-green wig to her head.

That night, dolled up in our sexy attire, I realized we still had it. *I still had it.* And that night, on my forty-seventh birthday, Paris made me feel younger and happier than I'd felt in months.

A parade of vaudeville entertainers—women rimmed in feathers and shirtless men—circled the room. While we tried to focus on the act, there was simply too much girl talk to be had.

"It's midnight!" Ang hollered. "It's your birthday!"

"It's your birthday! It's your birthday!" the Divas chanted.

I sank back in my chair and kicked up my heels. "Oh yes!" I said, clapping my hands. "What a wonderful day it is. Glad to be here another year! Thank you, Jesus! I'm so glad you ladies came along."

"Of course!" Brenda said. Then she looked right at me. "Gotta celebrate and be happy, right?"

"Right," I said, under a shower of confetti released by the venue. It felt surreal that the next day I would set off for Africa while my friends would continue on with four days in Spain.

"And what a ball *I* am having." Ang spoke to us, but her eyes were glued to a dark-haired man with olive skin and bulging biceps. Besides me, Angenette was the only single one on this trip. "There's no place I'd rather be," she said.

"What wouldn't you miss?" I asked her with a sneaky smile. "Sending me off, or his abs?"

"Both!" Mia chimed in on Ang's behalf.

We all laughed, a bit too loudly. When the four of us are together, our worries about work, home, children, and romance are all put aside.

"A toast to happiness," Angenette said, and raised her glass. Together we clinked glasses, taking in all the revelry.

"To happiness," I said.

I felt all the warmth and love of my friends surrounding me on my birthday. I didn't know how I'd feel the next day, but that night, that moment, was golden. And I saw myself as deserving of all the happiness that God had in store for me. He is the source of all joy, so it was okay for me to be happy.

Back in the hotel room that night, I felt some of my old fears returning. Had I made the right decision embarking

114

on this journey? Would I be safe? Was it worth the expense and time away? As I pondered these questions, there was no divine intervention warning me to give up my quest. Neither was there a voice from heaven saying, "Yes, Sheri, do it!" But I remembered how God had led me up to this point. I was reminded of the words of 1 Thessalonians 5:24: "The one who calls you is faithful, and he will do it." I could rest in that truth. Even with all I'd been through, God had never let go of me. And he wasn't about to now.

How do you discern where the Holy Spirit wants you to go? For me, it's not one prayer or two; it's a commitment to work toward understanding the Word and applying it to my life. Even when I make mistakes, I seek how to grow and learn from them.

•    •    •

The Divas sent me off in a theatrical way, and I couldn't help but be tickled. As we stood outside our Paris hotel hugging, saying our goodbyes, the Dare Divas crooned a Motown song. I'm not sure what the ballad was, but as the driver received my luggage from the curb and placed it into the trunk of the sedan, the Dare Divas kept singing and swaying. Folks stopped to watch them as they passed the hotel. Mia was right. People really did think we were something special.

In Paris, through the encouragement of my friends and our wild adventures, God gave me hope to dream again. He showed me the joy I had been missing for so long. Paris inspired me to be unflinching in pursuing both what I wanted in life and God's path for me. It encouraged me to get outside of myself and stop languishing in my grief. I knew the Lord had positioned me to be in this grand city with my dearest friends so I would begin to see myself the way he saw me—a bold woman who could chase my dreams. After all, the Creator himself didn't hold back in his creation of humanity and the world. He was and is the supreme visionary, and I am his child who can dream big too.

As my taxi pulled away from the hotel, the Dare Divas busted some dance moves. I waved from the back window, wishing I had thought to take a video to remember the farewell. There was, after all, sweet love in Paris. I kept my eyes fixed out the back window, and as the sedan began to turn the corner, I realized that my friends were there cheering me on until the very end.

# 6

# dare to move forward

## 65 days around the world . . . anointed

When Mannard was alive, he kept a colorful stack of cruise brochures in his home office, right next to his desk. While he paid our bills or filed important documents, he would often reach down and pick up the pile, riffle through it, and imagine setting sail on a luxury cruise liner to see the world.

One day a few months before he died, I stepped into his office, where he was absorbed by one particular pamphlet. "Have you seen this one?" he asked. "This ship goes all around the world, not in 60 days but 190—190, Sheri!"

I took the colorful Oceana pamphlet he handed me. On the cover, an aging couple strolled along a beach hand in hand.

"With this one cruise, we can visit all but one continent! I know it seems like a lot of money, but think about it. We'd only need to take one flight instead of the ten or twelve to visit each place separately."

I didn't want to spoil his dream. But really? We weren't elderly; we were in our forties. Didn't he know it would be a good fifteen or so years before we could make his dream a reality?

"Beautiful," I said. "So, when are we going?"

"I know," he said with resignation. "Not for some time. But we will go." He spoke with conviction, and I looked forward to the day we would take that trip.

Mannard called out after me as I left the office. "We can still get a glimpse of the good life for our twentieth anniversary. Remember that Holy Land tour?" Six years earlier, our former church had organized a trip to Israel, but we hadn't been able to go. "We can do something like that now," he continued, "but we can make it a cruise. A Holy Land cruise!"

"So no anniversary party?" I had secretly dreamed of renewing our vows for our twentieth anniversary. I thought we should do it while our parents were still living. The minister who had married us, who was also getting up in years, could do the honors.

"And pay for folks to eat for just one day?" he replied. "Nah. Let's do it up and get away for two whole weeks."

"Can we afford it?"

"Oh, baby," he said, taking my hand and swinging me into his lap. "We *is* going to the Holy Land!" Then he kissed me so hard I felt my lips tingle.

Mannard died six weeks before we were supposed to set sail on that cruise. Even though I knew he was in the true Holy Land and in the arms of the Almighty, removed from problems and pain, I couldn't rejoice. I felt heartsick that Mannard's post-retirement vision of sailing the world would never happen.

How could my heavenly Father be so cruel and take my beloved just before he tasted the fruits of his labor? I knew all things were possible for God, so why had he allowed this unexplainable tragedy to occur? In those early days after my husband's death, I forgot that God's wisdom is far beyond our human comprehension. He had specific ways he was going to use Mannard's passing in my life and in the lives of others.

After Mannard died, I considered tossing the brochures about the around-the-world cruises. But I couldn't bring myself to do that any more than I could toss his pair of prescription eyeglasses that I'd tucked in my bureau. When he'd last shown me those brochures, neither of us knew that he'd never retire, never see the kids graduate or go to college, never get to travel the world. His sudden death had darkened my world. It knocked me down. It crushed me. I spent months thinking through how I would live without him.

In July 2013, approaching the one-year anniversary of Mannard's death, I grew stronger and my grief was no longer as debilitating as it had once been. But I felt like I was lacking direction for the rest of my life. These years were supposed to be for Mannard and me, planning for our grand retirement. Instead, I was a single, working mama who desperately needed to know God's next steps for me.

• • •

So there I was on the trip of a lifetime, alone and feeling miserable.

By now I knew that the Dare Divas were in Spain, sightseeing for a few days before they returned home to Detroit. I would complete the next leg of my journey on my own. Before I set sail on my world cruise, I spent a few days in Johannesburg and Soweto to visit the haunts of people I admired. I visited Nelson Mandela's home and the Apartheid Museum only three weeks after the leader's death.

It was encouraging to take time to contemplate others who have weathered strife, turbulence, and the worst of times and somehow managed to come out with a positive and steadfast outlook on life. So many emotions overcame me as my hands brushed the red brick in the courtyard where bullet holes were made by opponents of integration. As I meandered through each small room, I could visualize Mrs. Mandela strategizing how to keep the children safe while her husband was imprisoned. Thinking of the troubles she must have endured and the courage required of her made my own troubles back in Michigan seem small by comparison.

The moment I set foot on Robben Island, I was enchanted. I know that may sound like a strange thing to say about the prison where Mandela was held for eighteen years. But take away the concrete prison, the barbed wire, and the security guard standing where I imagine an armed guard once stood, and it was a beautiful sanctuary.

At Robben Island, our tour guide—a former prisoner himself—guided us through a narrow passage devoid of electricity where scant natural light filtered through. We were led into what I could only describe as a holding room— rectangular, industrial, with benches around the perimeter. Next we entered Mandela's seven-by-nine-foot cinder-block cell, which had a simple mat on the floor, a brown blanket, a pillow, a small green side table, and a rusty steel bucket with a lid. My earlier impressions about the beauty of the place were replaced with horror. I felt deep sadness for what Mandela had endured there.

One thing I remember about his release from prison in 1990 was his determination to move forward and not allow himself to be stuck. When he could have become bitter about the twenty-seven years he'd "wasted" in prison, he rejoiced with great hope for the future. If Nelson Mandela could do that, then surely I could. I really wanted to.

In Soweto I ate *kasi kota*—hollowed-out bread filled with seasoned French fries, sauce, cheese, egg, and meat—a favorite of university students. I sampled *potjiekos* with dumplings and visited the vast parking lot of the FNB Stadium, home of the 2010 World Cup.

I got out of the car and twirled in the empty parking lot like I was in the opening scene of *The Mary Tyler Moore Show.*

"You are really getting into this," my driver, Douglas, said, eyeing me curiously.

"I just can't believe everything I've seen. I've dreamed about seeing these sights my whole life. It's all right here," I said in awe. I stopped in my tracks, realizing how silly I must have looked and sounded. "It's part of your culture." I shrugged. "You must be used to it."

Sensing my newfound modesty, Douglas grinned. "Yes, it is special. This is to be shared and enjoyed by everyone."

● ● ●

When I arrived in Cape Town, the Oceania cruise line provided a driver who held a sign with my name on it—a first for me. I grinned and pointed to the sign. "That's me," I said to the man who appeared to be of Indian descent.

"Welcome," the man said, introducing himself as Ben. He helped me gather my luggage, and soon we were in a car on our way to the ship. My visions of Africa—vast expanses of land with majestic animals—were elsewhere in this enormous continent. My view from the back of Ben's car showed me a modern city with skyscrapers and well-dressed people rushing around a thriving metropolis. The wind and warmth hugged me as I noticed Ben eyeing me curiously in the rearview mirror.

"How long are you working on the ship?" he asked with a South African accent.

"Working?" I said.

"Yes. How long will you be working on the ship?"

His meaning finally dawned on me. "No, sir," I said. "I'm not a worker. I will be a passenger on the ship for sixty-five days."

"Is that so?" Ben said, eyes wide. "God bless you and watch over you!"

What was a surprise to Ben was also a revelation to me. From this man's perspective, God was showering me with his favor. He was not accustomed to seeing a black woman traveling, or having the means to do so in such splendor. I felt a lump in my throat as I thought of God's goodness to me. He had brought me safely to Africa, and I believed that he would use the next sixty-five days to create something new in my life.

It was incredible to see God showing me his favor, protection, and grace. I know he can do this for you too, and I hope you will know it to be true when it happens.

. . .

I found my cabin on the grand ocean liner. Inside, I sank into the bed and let tears roll down my cheeks and into my pillow. I could hardly believe this was real. As a child, I had never traveled overseas. My diversions were parks or, on very special occasions, amusement parks. Now I was alone on Oceania's *Nautica* cruise ship. By the end of the sixty-five-day journey through Africa and Asia, I would visit more than twenty countries, including Kenya, Thailand, Maldives, Seychelles, and Hong Kong. My eyes would see so many ports that my beloved, Mannard, and I had planned to explore together.

My first real trip had been a cruise with Mannard. As an engineer at General Motors, he used part of his bonus toward a three-day cruise to the Bahamas. Oh, the joy of frolicking on the beaches together and rising in the morning to see Paradise Island on the horizon.

Now, as I bawled in my cabin, a part of me wanted to "get over" Mannard, like how you want to make a fresh start after a bad breakup. I wanted that sickening feeling to go away—that feeling where all you can think about is the other person, but you know being together will never happen. My love had been taken from me, and I felt like I would never get over the loss.

I probably could have sat in my cabin the entire sixty-five days, crying my eyes out into my pillow. But the ship's alarm blared inside my cabin, signaling that it was time to meet on deck for a mandatory safety demonstration. I heaved my legs over the side of my bed and went to wash my face in the small bathroom. I looked into my weepy eyes and spoke to

myself. "Girl, you can cry, but you got to keep it movin'."
This had become my mantra since Mannard had died. I knew
I needed to process my emotions, but no amount of crying
would bring him back. So even when I wanted to hide away
from others, my mantra got me going again.

I opened my cabin door, and a wave of light hit me. I
shielded my eyes. "Off to see the world," I said.

• • •

Even as I attempted to sail away from my grief and set a new
course, each day provided new thoughts of Mannard and fresh
pangs of grief. One of our first excursions was a tour of Dar es
Salaam, Tanzania. I sat inside a hut with a Maasai chief and his
six wives. "You can be number seven," he said with a wink.

Mannard would have cautioned the chief that I was a
handful and elbowed me in my ribs as we both laughed at
the outlandish offer. I could imagine him sitting cross-legged
on the dirt thatch floor of the hut, shaking hands with the
tribesmen and thanking the women who gave us juba juice
and plantains as a welcome. He would have looked upon the
lychee with suspicion at first but would have ended up peeling
it and taking a bite of the juicy, delicious fruit.

When we docked in Madagascar, children raced over to
make music for us, using sticks, rocks, and steel pots. These
little ones sang and danced their hearts out to generate
some income for their families. I felt Mannard's presence
as I placed a few dollars here and there, knowing there would
be more excursions like this one, more kids I would want to
give to. But as I walked away, I knew Mannard would have
reached inside his wallet, silently placed another five dollars
in their little buckets, smiled, and done it again.

Later that day, when a lemur leapt onto my shoulder and posed for a photo op, I pictured Mannard raising an eyebrow and saying, "That cute, furry creature could rip your throat out, you know." He would have warned me of the peril yet still aimed his camera to get the money shot, amused by his silly wife. I could imagine Mannard in each beautiful, new experience, and again my heart broke that he was not with me.

The adventure would have been breathtaking with Mannard. I imagined the joy I would have felt to see his face shining with glee over his plans manifesting. As I explored each port alone, I allowed the experience to wash over me—to seize me. And with the completion of each port, I whispered to my love, "Mannard, this is for you."

On the ship, I met other travelers from around the globe—Australia, Great Britain, Canada—and even four people who lived in Troy, Michigan, a mere three miles from my own home. We were strangers who had never laid eyes on each other, but here we were thousands of miles away on the same ship.

Not everyone on that ship was there for a vacation. Some, like me, had weathered difficult storms and were looking for a welcome escape from home. Janice and I were seatmates atop an elephant in Phuket, Thailand. A week later, over a cup of tea, I told her about Mannard's sudden death. Her expression clouded over, and she began taking shallow breaths.

"Are you okay, Janice?" I asked, concerned that she was having a health crisis.

"I'm fine," she said. "I'm so sorry to hear that, Sheri." Tears brimmed in her eyes. "I lost my son, Jeff, a year ago. He was forty-two."

"I'm so sorry, Janice," I said, taking her hand.

She choked back tears. "Sorry," she whispered. "I miss him so much, but I just can't talk about him right now."

We never spoke of Jeff again, and I understood. Though we were journeying to repair our hearts, true healing would take time. For the remainder of the cruise, the two of us simply enjoyed smiles and laughter with no talk of what we no longer had.

When I first boarded the ship, I learned that there was a once-a-week tea party for singles. The majority of the group was composed of women—most twenty years my senior. Not everyone was doing the sixty-five-day cruise. You could stay on the ship as long as 120 days, but many travelers joined for two weeks at a time.

Eight weeks in, we received a new crop of folks who joined us at Thailand and would sail with us through Singapore. Among the usual group of gray-haired ladies, there was one single male teeming with testosterone. Porter, a stockbroker from Melbourne, Australia, wore a suit over all six foot four of his athletic frame. Traces of his original blond hair peeked through thick whitish-gray.

"Ah, tea and coffee." He raised his teacup and flashed a warm smile. "Wouldn't it be nice to have something a little stronger to go with it? A shot of something to stir the blood? It *is* past noon."

"We've been thinking of switching it up a bit," said Katy, the events director for singles. "Maybe cocktails instead of tea. But it's hard to pass up the tea with the sandwiches and desserts."

Most of the ladies seemed taken with Porter. They leaned in a bit closer, hanging on his every word. I smiled in amusement but didn't share their crush. Mannard had been gone for only a year and a half, and I had no desire to engage in anything but banter as we compared travel stories.

The next morning as I worked out on the elliptical machine, sweat pouring down my face, Porter affixed himself to the elliptical next to mine. He was clad in new Nike attire, unlike my drab, well-worn gray workout pants.

"If you're like me," he said, "you're working like a wildcat to stave off the fatty five-course dinners." He smiled as his machine began whirring.

"I don't want to be as wide as the ship," I said, giving him a half smile. "If what they say is true, that guests gain five pounds for each week they're on the ship, they'll need a forklift to hoist me off like they do the cargo."

He grinned and leaned over as he ran. "Never will happen. You have a fine figure."

I tried my best not to act surprised. I was unaware that Porter had been sizing me up.

"We should have a drink, or maybe dinner," Porter offered.

I tried to breathe gracefully but failed. "Sure, we can," I said, puffing. "Who else should we invite to join in?"

Porter smiled. "No one else, just you and me."

I was perplexed. Porter was flirting with me. I quit running and looked him in the eye. I told him the truth—that I just wasn't ready.

Back in my cabin, I gathered my pillows and cried heartily for a couple of hours. Then I grabbed my journal. In big, bold letters I wrote, "GUILT."

Mannard should be here. This had been his dream. He was the one who had collected Oceania cruise brochures. He had a binder full of information about worldwide cruises. He had planned that we would take this adventure *together*.

As I wrote feverishly, swiping away at tears, one Scripture came to mind—Proverbs 3:5–6. I wrote it down, giving myself permission not to question this road. "Trust in the LORD with all your heart and lean not on your own understanding; in all your ways submit to him, and he will make your paths straight."

Submitting to the Lord is not as easy as it sounds. At least not for me. There have been things I wanted with all my heart—for Mannard to live, for one—but it was not part of God's plan. We will all have times like these in our lives where submission to God's will feels a lot more like heartbreak, but it's in those times that he makes our hearts more like his.

• • •

In Vietnam, I joined two other travelers—Aggie from Texas and Lisa from New York—and visited an open-air market where a pig limb hung on display like a prize. I shuddered to think about the germs and bacteria such conditions could introduce.

Market vendors offered samples of grilled meat with vegetables. I took one of the toothpick skewers and gobbled it down.

"You do know that was snake," Lisa said.

I nearly choked. "It is?!" The meat had tasted pretty decent, but I was not accustomed to eating reptiles.

"It's just like any other meat, Sheri," Aggie said. "You'll live."

I wasn't sure I agreed, but her words reminded me of everything I had come through since Mannard's death—how much I'd had to absorb. Many events had taken me by surprise, but as I took them in small bites, God allowed me to absorb them. My grief had not defeated me. Here I was, living and experiencing new things.

On the ship, I would sit on a lounge chair by the pool and write about all I was experiencing. But as I detailed each activity, each turn in the path so far beyond my life in Detroit, my writing became my enchanted solitude—a place to process my unfolding story and find meaning in it. Was it possible the Lord was revealing that writing was part of my future? With pen and paper, I began pouring out a story of deep loss, friendship, and dares that were elixir to my soul and helped me live again.

*   *   *

On my last day of the cruise, with our ship in the last port, we visited the Great Wall of China. After sixty-three days, I had literally made a boatload of friends. I had bonded with Tonya, one of the show dancers, who was a good fifteen years younger than me. We decided to tackle the Great Wall together.

"Oooh, that's some mama of a hike," Tonya said as we stared up at row after row of stone block stairs that seemed to be winding up past the clouds.

I sighed heavily, already feeling winded as I looked at the climb ahead.

"If the mountain don't come to Mohammed, then Mohammed goes to the mountain," Tonya said. We'd paid to take this journey, and we both really wanted to do it.

"Let's gird our loins and get to it," I said, laughing.

A few fit folks were already jogging past us.

"Hope they don't break anything, running like they're crazy up those steps," Tonya said. "That would be awful."

"Man, that would be bad." I was genuinely thankful that for all the days I'd traveled so far from home, I had not become ill or needed medical attention even once.

Three hours into our hike, miles and miles of the wall still remained. With each picture I snapped of the breathtaking, mountainous view, I realized that although this journey was coming to an end, a new one—a fresh start—would be waiting when I got home. On this trip there had been bouts of sadness, times when the walls felt like they were closing in, and I'd missed Mannard so badly that an outsider would have thought he'd passed away the day before. But this trip also marked a turning point for me. I was overcome with the assurance that God wanted me to keep moving forward even though Mannard was gone. There would be challenges, sure, but God would be with me through it all.

Up ahead, I saw the tallest of the towers. I began to walk faster, racing toward it.

"Wow, Sheri! What's the hurry?" Tonya said, picking up her pace to keep up with me.

"I have to get to the top of it," I said. I was breaking a sweat but not breathing as heavily as I felt I should be. I was jogging with ease. "I want to pray there before I leave."

Eight minutes later, I reached the base of the tower. I began climbing a series of tiny steps to reach the house at the top of the tower, but I tripped on a step and twisted my foot.

The narrow steps were so tight that Tonya found a way to get to the house much better—she crawled. "This must have been the torture section," she said, inching her petite frame up the stairs and past where I was standing. "I can barely fit."

I crawled after her and met her at the top. When I stood, I couldn't catch my breath. The expansive view was intoxicating. As I turned 360 degrees to take in the landscape around me, the beauty and grandeur of the Great Wall overwhelmed me.

Tonya and I shared a celebratory hug, and I smiled—no tears, just happiness. I stretched out my arms toward the heavens. And inside I whispered, *Thank you, Jesus. Thank you.*

That cruise was certainly a journey, and one I will never forget. I know that not everyone can pack up and venture out for sixty-five days. This had been a door of opportunity the Lord had opened for me, and I walked through it. Most times when I feel like the world is crashing over me and I need to escape outside my own environment, I can't go on a two-month cruise to a destination of my liking. I need to utilize the resources I have and move toward my well-being.

The movie *War Room* showed that when being attacked spiritually, you can stand still where you are and fight the battle. The title character, Elizabeth Jordan, was facing a disconnection from her husband, and her life was coming apart. What did she do? She used a closet in her home to commune with the Lord, and she went there regularly for time to pray, study, reflect, and nourish her soul. In the military, a war room is a place where military personnel gather to strategize for a specific mission, equipping themselves to win the battle. The same was true with Elizabeth—she was fighting for her family, she had the armor of the Lord, and she was set to win.

People in the Bible often sought solitude with God. Even Jesus did. He knew that living on earth has its beauty, but there are also overwhelming pressures, burdens, and temptations that can sway us away from God and the life he wants us to live.

Jesus was fully aware that he would suffer and die on the cross, so that walk toward the cross was an enormous one. He was sacrificing his life for the salvation of the world, and it would be brutal. Imagine facing that. Even though he was fully God as part of the Trinity, he was a man with flesh. His soul, his spirit, needed the comfort of his heavenly Father.

Just like you and me when we go through the unthinkable, Jesus had to get his mind positioned for the journey ahead. He went to the garden of Gethsemane, and there in solitude he communed with our Father and prayed for sustenance of the spirit as he moved toward the path of crucifixion. That wasn't the only time Jesus did this. He regularly had special times where he got away. Away from the world, people, and their problems, with his eyes solely on the one who held the entire universe in his hand.

If Jesus needed that time of solace, then we can see how we need it as well. And we can find our solace in somewhere special in our home, out in nature, walking with praise and worship music, in our vehicles as we drive, or wherever we feel most comfortable and ready to be vulnerable with the Lord. Wherever that may be, our Savior will meet us where we are.

• • •

By the end of the cruise, I was certain I wanted to live—not just to breathe but to move with intention, to be bold with expectations. On one of our last nights on the ship, I stood on the bow alone. Like in a scene from the movie

*Titanic,* I took in the view of the open ocean. I was alone, but there was a love story to be told. At every port, on every excursion, even in the quiet of my cabin where I cried into my pillow, Mannard had been there. He had left an indelible mark on me, and I knew he was now living in the fullest sense of the word.

I was learning that the greatest love story—even greater than the one Mannard and I had shared—was between Christ and me. He was giving me strength and teaching me to love the woman he had created me to be. In this way, my solo adventure was a gift. It was a joy to discover that I already had everything I needed to move forward, grow, and excel.

The wind whipped across my face and tousled my hair as the ship cruised through choppy waves, heading for our final port. I smiled. Even though this journey was ending, I felt ready for the journey that awaited me at home. Whatever problems I faced back in Michigan, God would help me prevail.

"I am a strong girl," I yelled into the wind. "I'm a Jesus girl!"

I stretched my arms wide and let a wave of gratefulness wash over me. Jesus was the one who had allowed this voyage and accompanied me on it. "Thank you, Lord," I whispered to my Savior. Though my face was wet with tears, I was no longer sad. I called out once again to love. "For you, Mannard. And for you, Jesus."

# 7

# dare to stay on course

## NASCAR, friends, and avoiding a crash

Nearly three years had passed since Mannard's death, and with the passing of time came inevitable changes. Mia moved to Charlotte, North Carolina, to take a new job. I had two kids in college. Angenette was in a serious relationship with the man she would eventually marry. And Brenda was preparing to send two kids off to college and become an empty nester. What had not changed was the deep friendship that had begun in 2005 and had lasted more than a decade.

The Dare Divas were also getting noticed by others. I had written an article for *More* magazine about Mannard and the unique friendship I'd formed with the Dare Divas through our death-defying challenges. And word was getting out. People followed us on our website and through social media. They seemed excited to see what crazy things these four black women from Detroit would do next. I got a glimpse of the impact we were having when a local Zumba instructor asked us to be part of her class. When we announced we were doing it and invited others to join us, sixty women signed up!

God had been working in my heart, showing me that maybe this whole Dare Diva thing was bigger than I imagined. Maybe he was going to use our friendship to inspire countless others to be brave and move boldly toward the life God had for them.

In the spring of 2015, I had reached out to TV stations in Detroit and Charlotte. The producers at FOX in Detroit loved the story of triumph over loss with adventurous feats and good friends, and they invited us to come to the studio for an interview.

On the morning of our interview, the four of us giggled in the greenroom.

"We are about to be on TV!" Mia said. "Ahhhh! Can you believe this?"

I looked in the mirror, adding an extra coat of mascara and touching up my lip color.

"This is so cool. Everyone at home is taping it," Brenda said, adding a spritz of hairspray.

"Yeah," I said, looking at my reflection in the mirror. I adjusted my sparkly Dare Diva shirt. "Wow, maybe I should have worn Spanx. I hear the cameras add ten pounds."

Angenette smiled at my reflection. "You look great. We all look great."

On air, we were fired up.

"And that's how I got stuck on the zip line and hovered four hundred feet above ground!" Mia said, her eyes wide. The interviewer, Taryn Asher, had just asked us to talk about our scariest dare.

"And you guys went whitewater rafting and couldn't swim?" Taryn laughed, and we all chuckled at the absurdity of that.

"Yes, we did! But we had life jackets," Angenette explained.

"Safety first."

Angenette shared that she had invested in swim lessons in the past but they never stuck; in fact, she was still traumatized by a bad dive she'd taken in her last class. I couldn't swim either, so I couldn't save myself in a huge body of water. Mia and Brenda had some swimming skills, though I didn't know how much. Caught up in the moment, they just nodded, smiled, and went along with the story.

"So, what's your next feat?" Taryn asked.

"Scuba diving," Brenda said.

"And can others come along?" she asked.

"Oh, sure!" Ang said.

"The more the merrier!" I added.

Our first TV appearance seemed to be a hit, but Taryn's question about including others in our dares had us thinking. The Dare Divas had taken on a life of its own. Clearly what God had done through us as a group was bigger than any one individual. Our friendship and antics inspired people. Women wanted to be like us, or at least be our friends.

After the interview, we settled in at a nearby Original Pancake House to discuss the group's future.

"Everyone keeps asking what's next," I said. "There is so much we can do. Should we create Dare Diva chapters? Should we sponsor a Dare Diva fund-raiser to benefit a group for inner-city girls?"

Mia nodded. "I can definitely see us doing more. If we want to make this Divas thing bigger so we can impact more people, I'm in!"

"I don't really want to do anything more than the dares," Angenette stated without hesitation. "This is fun for me, an escape. I don't want to turn it into a business."

I was surprised by her response. Why was she against doing more? Was it because she was already overwhelmed with work and dealing with her ailing mom? I didn't press the matter, because she clearly had a strong opinion.

Brenda sighed and nodded. "If I had more time, more energy, I would be down. But with preparing the kids for college, life in general is more than full enough for me right now."

Mia looked down at her phone. "Well, we are getting likes and comments on the Dare Diva Facebook page. People want to know how they can join in."

"I do get questions from coworkers all the time," Brenda said. "Maybe we can do some sort of activity locally."

Angenette gulped her coffee. "I'm good with doing something low-key. I can speak at churches, but I don't want to deal with groups of women we have to then *manage*."

"Maybe between the four of us we can divide and conquer?" I suggested. "We could start small—supporting charities that focus on women or participating in local youth programs that get kids exercising. Maybe the Lord wants us to help others by doing *more* than just the dares." I tried not to sound bossy.

As the flurry of interest developed, there was concern about how others could use our image, our names, and even the Dare Diva name we had created. The four of us drew interest from others who thought the dares were fun and cool, and to our surprise there were now numerous women who were inspired and wanted to join in.

Angenette spoke with a colleague who specialized in trademark law about acquiring the Dare Diva name legally. Angenette was a seasoned corporate attorney with nearly twenty years of experience, so it was second nature for her to act as good shepherd over our legal interests. At that time, she had climbed the ranks at both law firms and corporations, had become a senior counsel at a Fortune 500 company, and was licensed to practice law in two states. After completing our initial trademark filing, she coordinated our engagement of trademark counsel and kept us informed throughout the entire registration process. As a result of her good foresight and diligence, Dare Divas International LLC was formed and our trademark strategy was solid.

Mia and Brenda both contributed greatly to the Dare Diva venture as well. Mia diligently worked side by side with her cousin to develop our website. They spent time investigating, designing, and purchasing merchandise we could sell—T-shirts, mugs, and all kinds of things with the Dare Diva logo beautifully displayed on them. Brenda faithfully responded to the surge of comments and questions on our Facebook page and engaged her talented sister-in-law to create our eye-catching Dare Diva logo. I secured our website and reached out to TV stations and media outlets to get on local morning shows in Detroit and Charlotte. With my background as a TV news producer, I knew this would be a hot story.

Together, the four of us sat down and wrote our vision and mission statements. We each had concerns about money and the investment, but we plugged along.

It was so wonderful to see us all come together as the strong, confident, intelligent women we were in business. Angenette was using her legal skills; Mia, who was vice president of auditing with an international banking institution, was using her organizational skills and attention to detail; and Brenda, who worked in management in public health and was herself a business owner of an insurance agency with her husband, was vocal about matters that would help us as a group and others who were interested in joining in.

As things began to churn, my stomach became queasy when I recalled a recent sour business deal. Mannard and I had lost thousands in an investment with a friend. That person was wise, talented, and connected and had an excellent idea that Mannard and I believed in. When Mannard died, I was left to shepherd that bad decision. It was based on emotions instead of making sure there was a business plan that was actionable and achievable.

Like with that deal, there were now lots of wonderful dreams, like the idea of having Dare Diva chapters around the world. And there was a lot of energy to ramp up, with cash outlay activities to get websites, trademarks, and logos. But exactly how would we recoup our investment?

As the other Divas were power players outside of our Dare Diva activities, I knew they were cognizant of cost too. They cared, and they didn't want their investment to be for naught. After weathering a major loss, I was highly sensitive to not having a plan. I didn't want to make another investment without having a clear picture of where we were going. Capital outlay, desires, and dreams were not a plan, and that scared me.

As we were discussing merchandising at my house, what to purchase, and how much, I spoke up. "Guys, you know what went down with a previous deal. I'm just feeling uncomfortable with us not having a plan of how to recoup this money I'm spending."

This was a rare time when I was vulnerable and shared a private fear. I didn't do that lightly, and I hoped the ladies would hear my heart and tell me either they would work to develop a plan or they would keep it real with me and admit they didn't have the time, desire, or interest to do more. Having that information would aid me in how I would operate going forward.

"What you're saying about planning makes sense," Brenda said. "We should talk more. It's just hard when we don't know exactly where this is going."

"I know that situation caused you a lot of hurt, Sheri," Ang said. "But this is different. This is about protecting the Dare Diva name. The one *we* created. And we need to protect that before we do anything else."

Her argument was solid, but I still wanted to know how each of us would be contributing to the overall success of the Dare Divas once we had spent the money. "What comes next other than writing checks?" I asked. I felt in my spirit that handing over the check I'd just written was the right thing to do, but I was also starting to wonder if being in business with these women would jeopardize the special bond we had formed.

"I don't know," Mia said as she gave me a pointed look.

Neither of the other two spoke up, and I took it as a three-against-one affront. I was hurt. I felt ignored. Worse than that, I felt manipulated. It seemed as if my friends had formed an alliance, only holding the meeting to pacify me so they could do what they wanted.

I ultimately agreed to move forward with the belief that we would equally contribute to marketing and getting the word out to inspire and possibly generate revenue, which we could give to nonprofits or whatever we desired. We each had worked hard, and I needed solid plans and the confidence of a good investment.

A good two weeks later when once again I found myself in the same situation—paying funds but having no official meetings to discuss plans or how we would move forward—I felt my friends had intentionally ignored my viewpoint and that my feelings once again didn't matter. Later that evening, I was seething with anger. The more I thought about our conversations, the more I felt unappreciated for my contributions to our popularity. I was the one who had written the articles and reached out to the TV stations. I still loved these women deeply, but I was irritated with them. I had to figure out what was going on. Was it them or was it me?

I wondered if Satan was attempting to drive a wedge in our sisterhood and friendship. He liked to mess up a good thing. Yet I also wondered if our friendship had reached its natural end. It seemed we each wanted different things out of life. I craved having greater impact on people's lives through the platform God had provided. In fact, as more and more opportunities came my way, I felt like he'd shown me this was the path for me. But the other girls seemed content to let our adventures be a fun hobby and nothing more.

I tried not to let the relational drama weigh me down. I didn't want to think the worst of my friends. Maybe I was being too sensitive. Our next dare was coming up, and though the ladies were getting excited, I was still angry.

We had planned to make scuba diving our next dare, but none of us had learned to swim or earned the necessary dive certifications. With Mia residing in North Carolina, we decided to take a little trip to visit her and have our next dare at the NASCAR Racing Experience in Charlotte. During this bucket-list experience, we would receive training and instruction from professionals and end our day by driving a race car solo during a timed racing session. With no lead car or instructor in the passenger seat and only two-way radio communication, the simulation would be realistic and daring.

Once the NASCAR dare was on the calendar, the Divas couldn't stop talking about it. While I wanted to join in their excitement, I was hesitant to be around the women who had hurt my feelings so much. I reread our group text message exchange, hoping to channel some of their energy.

**Mia**
We have our tickets. Only two months away. Yay!

**Angenette**
🏎️ 👏 💥 Ricky Bobby ain't got nothing on us.

**Brenda**
I am uber excited. Can't wait to race to the finish.

I remained silent. I was beginning to feel that if I went to Charlotte with my current attitude, it wouldn't be pretty. I'd like to say that I searched the Scriptures on verses about love, friendship, and peace, but I didn't. I opted to be petty.

I texted the group.

Dare Divas, I'm going to chill for a while, need to just get my life together. I'm going to pass this time.

**Mia**
Are you saying you're not doing the dare? You're not doing NASCAR?

Nope. Not this time.

My full response played out inside my head: *No, I'm not going to do any NASCAR dare with y'all because you're getting on my nerves! I can't just act like everything's okay.*

Brenda and Angenette didn't respond, and it's probably best they didn't. Maybe they were feeling like I was. Sometimes a hushed mouth is best. James 1:19 says, "My dear brothers and sisters, take note of this: Everyone should be quick to listen, slow to speak and slow to become angry." That's what I was feeling. I needed to guard my tongue so I didn't hurt anyone.

Have you ever said something and later regretted it? Words can haunt you, and the wound of those words can linger long after apologies have been extended. I wanted to avoid that, and as hard as it was, I worked to avoid causing damage with my words.

Looking back, I don't think the other Divas were against shepherding our brand in an organized way like I'd suggested. Maybe it just wasn't the right time. They each were likely going through their own personal struggles with work, family, and relationship demands.

I realized that I had no control over their thoughts or actions, but I did have control over mine. I could not let the enemy take hold of my spirit or tempt me to harm my friends by bad-mouthing them or spreading hurtful gossip. I prayed for God to be my defender and mend my bruised spirit.

## DECEMBER 2015

When the other Divas proceeded with the NASCAR dare without me, social media blew up with the splendor of Mia, Brenda, and Angenette speeding down the Charlotte Motor

Speedway. As I sat in my office sipping my coffee, I had to admit that I missed being with them. I had let my pride get in the way of having fun.

It's harder to swallow your pride when you're not entirely in the wrong. How does one go about sharing when a boundary has been crossed without fracturing the relationship? Maybe you've struggled with that as I have.

I knew in my heart that we could have worked it all out. I knew I could have been more patient and spoken with more kindness. But I wasn't the only one at fault for our rift. It can be humbling to realize that, despite our own hurt emotions, we've hurt someone else in return. Claiming that offense and being intentional about healing the division takes hard, persistent work.

The Dare Divas had been there for me during my darkest hours. And I had been there for them too. We had taken on one another's hardships and rallied around one another during our most trying times. Whether it was the deaths of loved ones, illnesses, career challenges, parenting struggles, or the dating woes of us single Christian women, we had seen each other through many victories and defeats. When one of us needed a friend, the others had showed up. We brought each other meals, cleaned each other's houses, brought over a bag of groceries, or just sat listening, holding a Kleenex to wipe away wayward tears. These beautiful souls had been a safe harbor in the storms of life and became more like family than friends.

But this time the storm was different. It wasn't a challenge that came from the outside; it was a cancer that had infected our group. Our disunity seemed to tap into the ugly parts of our humanity—ego, pride, haughtiness, and careless words. I learned that being a friend can be uncomfortable, even awkward. At times the effort may not seem worth it. In those moments, we have to set aside our own feelings, be patient, and really listen.

The first time we encountered a major disagreement, we allowed ourselves to become divided over it instead of embracing each other as we had done before. When the other three banded together, I felt betrayed.

Those feelings were compounded when the girls appeared on the local FOX affiliate in Charlotte the day after the NASCAR dare. It was the same station I had reached out to for an earlier Diva interview. There they were once again, only this time they were appearing without me.

"I hear the NASCAR experience was amazing," the host, Caitlin Lockerbie, gushed. "Sheri, where are you? You should be here."

I felt guilty for being a no-show. Our social media followers were also asking why I wasn't there.

Mia, Angenette, and Brenda were lined up in a row, wearing their matching black Dare Diva tees. From what I had seen, they looked amazing racing down the Motor Speedway. They had posed in their blue fire-retardant suits with the pink tees underneath, and they looked not just cute but like attractive, sassy Christian women.

"I was a nervous wreck," Mia told the host, "but I pushed through. That's what we do for one another—we motivate each other to push through our fears."

Her statement was like a knife to my heart. At the moment, that was the last thing I felt like the Divas had done. In my mind, they'd turned on me when I voiced my fears. Instead of helping me push through, they'd dismissed my concerns.

"We miss you, Sheri," each Diva said on air. But I secretly wondered if they really did.

I turned off the TV and sat back in my chair. Despite my hurt and disappointment, there was no question in my mind that Brenda, Angenette, and Mia were amazing women. I reflected back on our years of extraordinary friendship. We had shared so many good times—mostly good times. Though the painful emotions I was experiencing in this season seemed so powerful, I wasn't ready to chuck the friendship entirely, and I hoped they felt the same.

At some point in every meaningful relationship we have, someone will say or do something that hurts us. No spouse, parent, sibling, or child is perfect. We all say hurtful words or cross boundaries that can damage relationships. But if we value the relationship, we realize it's worth fighting for.

I remembered a time when Mannard and I exchanged some particularly unkind words. I was engulfed in the stress of caring for young children, and I felt like he wasn't supporting me enough.

He had just loaded the dishwasher and was heading to our room to take a nap, while I had taken care of the laundry and fed our two- and three-year-olds. I was fed up and felt like I was doing everything.

"You can help a bit more with the kids, you know," I said. "I have a full-time job too."

"Excuse me," he fired back. "I do my part. Many women would be *thrilled* to have a man who contributes like I do. Neither of our fathers did. You should be happy."

*Why did he have to say that?* I turned on my husband and gave him a withering look. "Mister, just because we had fathers who dropped the ball doesn't mean you get a pat on the back for being a 'good enough' father. You are *supposed* to do that. You get no awards."

To this day, I'm pretty sure that conversation ended up being the most painful and heated argument we had ever had. We didn't make up before going to bed, like all those marriage books suggest. He stayed on his side and I stayed on mine.

It was only the next morning when I was brushing my teeth that my heart softened. Mannard was bathing David, singing and laughing. He wrapped our son in a fluffy towel before leaning over to kiss my cheek. "I'm sorry. You were right. I'll do better. I was just tired."

"No, I wasn't right, and you weren't wrong," I said. "We're in this together. It's okay to be tired. We just need to tell each other when we need a break."

That wasn't the only time our stress or selfishness caused us to speak harsh words and hurt each other's feelings, but we always made sure to make up after that. We loved each other and realized we were better for having the other in our lives. I would never have considered giving up on my husband over a stupid fight, no matter how hurt I was. Perhaps I needed to offer the Divas the same benefit of the doubt.

●　●　●

Although I didn't share the NASCAR experience with the Divas, I did have my own turn on the track. When the idea of the NASCAR dare first came up in February of that year, I mentioned it to David and Danielle on one of our Friday night family dinner dates.

"Mom, that dare has swagga!" David said. "Like Jay-Z style. I gotta do *that*!"

"You want to do it, huh?" I said, feeling pretty special that David considered his old mom's antics cool. "We old gals can still show you kids a thing or two."

"Well, yeah," he said, taking a bite of his calamari. "You got it going *on*, Mom. And I know you won't disappoint. Turn up! Let's go!"

David's twenty-first birthday was coming up in June, so we made plans to take to the track together to celebrate his big day.

I chuckled. "Yes, we are gonna 'turn up,'" I said, incorporating my son's slang for *party time*. "I'm gonna turn it all the way up!"

"As much as you can with your mama," Danielle said with a wry smile.

"Don't hate," David said. "I know Mom will make my birthday big!"

"You know I won't let you down," I said. "You're gonna be a man, so we're going to set this new life on fire."

"I won't be in town," Danielle said with resignation. She would be in DC for a summer internship, which included working weekends. "I'm not mad, though. Whatever you get for your birthday, mine will be just as bad. If your birthday is fire, mine will be liquid propane!"

## AUGUST 2015

Our racing experience would not be in Charlotte but at the Chicagoland track in Joliet, Illinois. There David and I donned our royal-blue NASCAR suits and helmets. We were practically bursting with excitement, ready to tackle this dare together.

"We are going to do this, Mom," David said. "Look at those whips!" He pointed to some shiny race cars, and in that instant I saw him as a five-year-old little boy seeing the bumper cars at the amusement park for the first time. That day so many years ago, his sweaty little hand had grabbed mine and pulled me along for his chance to "drive." I had ridden shotgun.

The Chicagoland track was awe-inspiring. We stood with our hands on the track rails like two wide-eyed kids watching the grown-ups doing things we had only dreamed of doing—except we would be doing those very same things in only thirty minutes!

During the preride instruction session, my son's excitement turned to worry as the instructors gave us detailed instructions on how to handle a 3,300-pound vehicle at high speeds.

"Yo, Mom, I can't do this," David said to me quietly, his eyes wide. "I don't know how to drive a stick shift."

An instructional board in front of us displayed an image of the inside of the vehicle dashboard and instructions for shifting the gears. I was suddenly panicking along with David. I knew how to drive a stick, but he had never been trained on it.

I tried to hide my concern. "They will teach you," I said, trying to sound reassuring. "And if it's too much for you, you can just sit in the passenger's seat and ride along."

The race experience provided two options. In option one, you rode shotgun alongside an instructor. In option two, you drove solo. I paid for us to do both, first as passengers, then as drivers.

I waited nervously on the sidelines while David rode around the track with the instructor. As he completed his lap, I was prepared to encourage David to just do another ride as a passenger rather than driving solo. I figured it was better to be safe than sorry.

"Are you kiddin' me?" David said when I made the suggestion. "No way! I'm driving, Mom. I'm going to shift, and drive. The instructor says it will be fine."

David introduced me to his instructor, Moe, a giant of a man. He was a good six foot five and had twenty-two years of experience as a NASCAR instructor.

"I gave him some pointers," Moe said. "And he demonstrated to me that he can do it."

We had already signed the necessary waivers, but even with Moe's assurance, I wasn't confident. *What would Mannard do?* I thought. When I found myself in a quandary, not certain what decision to make, I'd always think of Mannard.

"David, you're not driving solo," I said. I did what I was certain Mannard would do, only I didn't get the response his gruff paternal voice always induced.

"I'm doing it, Mom. Remember, I'm twenty-one," David said. Then he positioned himself in the driver's seat and gave me a thumbs-up before putting the car in gear and taking off.

I prayed as I slid into my own driver's seat. "Please, Jesus, let us all be safe today. No injuries. No crashes."

There would be eight of us on the track. From the holding area, I eased into a lane, switched gears, and accelerated down the track. Soon I was speeding toward a 170-degree curve with the speedometer reading 115 miles per hour. My jowls were flapping, and my hands had a death grip on the steering wheel. I saw my competitors just ahead on the track. If I revved the engine, I might be able to inch past them and win the challenge. But if I veered off course (novice that I was), I could spin out of control, T-bone another car, or collide with the retaining wall.

I didn't have enough professional knowledge to know the delicate balance between high-performance racing moves and rookie mistakes that could lead to a crash. I lacked the skills and steely nerves of a NASCAR champion. I decided that slowly easing into the curve was the best solution for me. It was the only way I could see beyond the danger zone while still maintaining control of the 3,300-pound beast in my hands.

That August afternoon, I didn't focus on those cars just a smidgeon ahead of me on the track, which were taking the curve a bit faster than I was comfortable doing. I stayed in my lane, making judgments that fit my own mental capacity. I reduced my speed to 105 miles per hour around the curve. Though I was driving slower, it still felt mad fast, like a rocket. The highest I had ever accelerated to was 80 on a freeway with a speed limit of 60 miles per hour, and a state police officer made me regret it.

On the Chicagoland track there was no penalty for speeding—it was welcome. But snug within the steel-framed compartment, I was only going to go as fast as I allowed myself. I eased off the accelerator through the curve, easily speeding through the 90-degree angle that could have wiped me out. I put my foot on the gas and accelerated to 110, then 115 on lap two. I'm sure my blood pressure was surging too, as my emotional state was equal parts exhilaration and terror. Who was I?

I was in fifth place out of eight racers, but I wasn't going out easily. Not that day. My whole body vibrated as my speed topped out at 120 around lap two, where I easily passed a fellow racer. On lap three, I was neck and neck with another driver in a tricked-out blue Chevy. I kept my speed steady and let him eat my dust.

When all was said and done and the dust settled, I came in second. I pumped my fist and thumped the steering wheel. Then I shifted into second gear as the NASCAR crew member waved me over. The ride of my life came to a close, and as I brought the mighty race car to a halt, my heart sank a bit. When the crew member opened the door, I sighed and kept my hands on the wheel, feeling the space, allowing the vibration to shake me once more, before I exited the vehicle.

David was getting out of his car when he saw me coming. He ran to me, and we shared a triumphant embrace.

"Mom, that was the bomb!" he said. "I got up to 120. 120! Best birthday so far!" His grin filled me with joy.

I hugged him again and didn't want to let go. "I'm glad, Son. I'm so, so glad."

* * *

After the Divas' NASCAR dare, things were still strained between us. Brenda set up a conference call for us to discuss the website.

"According to the designer, the website is nearly complete," she said. "But we still need to think about merchandising. That will give us some solid protections should anyone want to use or acquire our brand."

The previous week, I had let everyone know that I would not spend money on the merchandising because we still hadn't created any sort of official business plan. How were we going to sell these shirts to people other than friends? What actions would we each do to recoup our investment?

"Well, Sheri," Angenette said, "that's not cool for you to back out."

Mia was not her usual bubbly self. "Yeah," she said. "That was not expected. And I really don't want to be in business like that."

"It was surprising and hurtful," Brenda said. "Especially when you'd agreed to it before."

Brenda's words cut deep, but I was grateful for her honesty in supplying a specific grievance. I had promised myself before the call that I would tell the girls my true feelings.

"You're right. It was unkind to switch things on you like that without any explanation. I did agree to the investment," I began gently. "I'm sorry. I will pay as I agreed."

Still, there were things that needed to be said. When a major corporation wanted to use our trademark and our names, we all collectively felt it was a bad deal. They basically wanted to use everything for free. Though we may have been four inner-city girls born with very little, we were now highly educated and pretty savvy. We politely, resoundingly declined the offer.

We still needed to have a conversation after that rejection. Moving forward, with the four of us likely having our own, individual ideas of what a good deal would look like, I felt it was important to share what we personally valued, what dollar amount would be satisfactory, and what points would dissatisfy and satisfy us.

I knew the negotiation had been wearisome. Angenette had graciously put in a lot of time negotiating for us, and she did this for free. We each had been hammered by the months-long back-and-forth. It was tiresome for me, and I was not the one engaging the dialogue with the other attorneys. But the deal was dead, and there was no offer in our impending future from anyone else.

When I inquired about further conversation following the declined deal, it was unwelcome. At the very least, no one else brought up the idea of next steps. During negotiations, all the information shared about the deal, all the endless effort and professionalism, were welcome, and I was thankful. We had conducted ourselves as highly skilled businesspeople. What was lacking was hearing a friend about the importance of having some kind of marketing or business plan. My fear was making an investment without any idea of how I would get a return. Not having communication or a viable plan was a recipe to lose money once again.

Though I didn't want to stir up trouble, remaining silent and fearful would mean I wasn't being the woman God created me to be. "Ladies, while I apologize, I will say this—I'm not the only one who should be apologizing." I breathed in deeply, because I was about to confront my friends personally. "Angenette, when you guys refused to talk further about our next steps, you treated us—you treated *me*—like an adversary. That's something an attorney does when a negotiation has gone bad. It's not how a person who loves you treats you. *That* was hurtful."

After a pause, Ang responded in a low voice with an apology. I could hear that she was hurt by my honesty.

"Ang, please hear me," I said. "No matter what we are going through in our personal lives, just like at our jobs when we're expected to perform no matter what, we have to be present and attentive to each other's questions and concerns. Yes, we're friends, but we're spending funds, investing in projects. And for a business partner—and yes, this is business we are in together—it's not unreasonable to expect regular communication and not feel like we are an irritant for asking questions. If any of us need a break, we need to say so."

Mia piped up. "Well, what about bailing on the NASCAR dare, Sheri?"

I didn't appreciate her insinuation that I'd done something wrong by not joining them. Each one of us had sat out at least one dare, and it wasn't part of our group vibe to make that person feel guilty about it.

I raised my voice, speaking sharply. "That was a dare, Mia. This is *business*! If you're talking about money—if we're writing checks—it's business!"

Everyone was silent.

I continued. "Mia and Brenda, I wanted to hear your individual thoughts on all this, not just the consensus. I shared that I had concerns about going into business with friends after having a bad experience, and you guys seemed indifferent." As I laid it all out there, I felt God's strength to speak the truth in love. "I'm sorry, but this is not all me."

Brenda spoke first. "Sheri, I'm sorry too. There were times I should have spoken up when I felt things weren't being done in a businesslike way. Honestly, I have just been so overwhelmed with my own life, I didn't want to address it. But you're right, that's not an excuse. I could have done better."

"I'm sorry too," Mia said slowly. "There were things done intentionally and some by mistake. I know it was wrong, and I'm sorry."

Angenette was the last to speak. I think she was still smarting from my frank declaration. I wondered if I had been too harsh.

"I'm sorry too," she finally said softly.

We ended the call. That conversation was not pleasant, and I believe the only reason it did not end our relationship is because we did not attack each other or speak hate-filled words. I have been guilty of that in the past, but I managed to steer clear of it this time. Taming the tongue is one of the hardest things to do, but also the most beneficial.

What was certain was that God had shown us how to weather a storm. It was not by using foul language, name calling, spreading vicious rumors about each other, hurling objects, or placing our hands on each other. As Christians, we are commanded to speak in love, not withdraw or run away from a problem. Speak. In love.

It took several weeks after that to get back to our usual banter and affection. But within a few months, I discovered that we were each in this sisterhood for the long haul. We valued our friendship enough to work through the uncomfortable stuff. Like before, we began reaching out to the group for prayer when we faced different challenges. We even began planning for our next dare.

"It's time, Dare Divas," Angenette said one day. "It's time to climb Mount Kilimanjaro. We can do this."

"Time to climb that mountain," I said, looping my arm around my friend.

The Dare Divas were back! We gathered together and began to dream about our greatest dare yet.

• • •

When I was on that NASCAR racetrack, I was very aware of the power of that car. It was hard to be in control of the vehicle unless I focused. At any moment, if I wasn't paying attention, it could veer off course or spin out of control, causing serious damage.

Relationships are a lot like that. If we don't give them the tender love, care, and attention they require, they can spin out of control or veer off in a direction we didn't anticipate. But like a race car, when steered properly, friendships can do amazing things. God didn't create us to go it alone on this earth. He gives us friends to encourage and challenge us.

I've learned that healthy friendships require vulnerability and give-and-take so both people feel the benefit of the relationship. I think that's what Proverbs 27:17 means when it says, "As iron sharpens iron, so one person sharpens another."

It also helps to have compassion and grace when those we love inevitably make mistakes. None of us are perfect. And our imperfect earthly relationships are going to hit bumps in the road. That's part of being human. We each come to relationships with our own history, baggage, and points of view. We each have our own unique way we want to be loved. When a friend disappoints us, we have the choice to put in the work of reconciliation, which requires humility and grace, or throw in the towel and move on.

The Dare Divas have cried with me and prayed with me. They've helped me to take crazy-big risks and bold steps I never imagined I could. Even when our friendship hit a rough patch in the road, God helped us steer back on course. I think that's what friendship is about—giving grace, forgiving, and moving forward together in sisterhood.

# 8

# dare to let go

up, up, and away in a beautiful balloon

"Don't make any hasty decisions!" said Joanne, a coworker of mine, as we talked over lunch about six months after Mannard had passed. A fellow widow, she had lost her husband five years before I lost Mannard.

"I just don't know if I can stay in the house where he died," I said. I wasn't sure whether to move or stay. I didn't even know if I could sell the house, as I currently owed the bank more than it was worth.

"Give yourself time." She patted my arm.

Joanne's husband had also died at home early in the morning. He passed away while getting ready for work. She had chosen to stay and live in the house where he had taken his last breath. She was strong enough to manage all the love and memories they shared in the house, along with the last haunting moments of her husband's life. I listened to

Joanne's opinion. She had done what I hoped to do: maintained her career, sent her son off to college, and even started dating again.

"You just don't know," she said. "You could be single for the rest of your life. And you don't want to have any regrets about poor financial decisions."

I hadn't even shared with Joanne the worst of it, like our mortgage being underwater and the kids' car being repossessed. I wondered at the ease with which it seemed she could move on and get her life back on track. Would I ever get there?

Mannard came to my rescue in death as he had in life. He'd left an insurance policy that gave the kids and me the financial freedom not to be destitute after his death, since he was the primary provider. Still, if managed improperly, the funds could easily dwindle to nothing. I had to grapple with how to keep my family afloat, make sure we had a roof over our heads, pay college expenses, and save enough for retirement. A series of bad investments, too many trips to the mall, or plain carelessness could torpedo all the hard work and smart planning my husband had done.

I sat at the kitchen table and anxiously eyeballed the Excel sheet Mannard had created that detailed our bills. I followed it to a T and made some conservative adjustments for those surprise home expenses that always arise. With proper management, we would still have a nice home, vacations, and even some grandeur now and then, but not more than what the budget allowed.

• • •

About four years later, in 2016, Joanne's words had not left me. *You could be single for the rest of your life.* Though

I had adapted to being an independent single mom, I wasn't positive I wanted to be single forever. At the same time, I had accomplished a lot in four years. I had negotiated a short sale on our beautiful home and found a smaller, cozier house that fit our family's needs. With the kids away at college, I truly was content with my new life. More than that, I felt downright empowered.

Although I no longer had Mannard, my partner, I wasn't alone. I had the Dare Divas. And I began branching out to make new friends. I joined an online meet-up group, where people with mutual interests could engage in group activities. I noticed they had done many of the same activities the Dare Divas had conquered together—skydiving, zip-lining, and whitewater rafting, to name a few. The group's next activity would be a hot air balloon ride.

The Divas and I had talked about taking a hot air balloon ride, but we hadn't ever settled on when it would work with our competing schedules. At that point, all of the other Divas had a significant other, which limited the scheduling of dares. I understood. I'd had less time for my single friends when I was married. There were activities I could have done with friends that I chose to do with Mannard. Now I was the odd girl out, but I got it. Relationships require a lot of time and energy to nurture. But I still wanted to go on a hot air balloon ride, and so did Brenda. We tried and tried for months but could not coordinate our schedules so that we could go on the same ride. We agreed to do the dare on different days but to be together in spirit.

I blasted Toby Mac and Vickie Winans from the speakers of my SUV on my way up to Fenton, Michigan, a city about an hour outside of Detroit. I was in good spirits as I coasted north up I-75, ready to take the journey, praying that God would protect me.

In the four years since Mannard had passed, I had changed to the point that I barely recognized myself. Who was this brave woman who wanted to participate in this thrill ride all by herself? Certainly not Sheri Hunter! And yet it was me. This new freedom I felt to move through life with confidence was so exhilarating. Instead of white-knuckling it all the time, I was learning to allow God to be the navigator of my life and correct my course when I got off track.

At Balloon Quest, I joined three couples and our flight crew near the takeoff point. A multicolored balloon lay flat on the ground. The massive piece of nylon stretched about half the length of a soccer field.

Our pilot, Mick, must have noticed our incredulous looks. "Don't worry," he said. "It may be flat now, but in a few minutes, you won't even recognize it."

Pete, our navigator, and six other men tugged at the edges of the balloon, pulling it taut.

"Gather around," Mick said, and the seven of us complied. "Be careful. It's hot."

He was right. I could feel the heat pumping from the inflator fan. I pulled out my cell phone to record the balloon's metamorphosis and stream it live to Facebook. As hot air began coursing through the panels of the balloon, the massive thing began to rise like a floppy bubble.

I aimed the camera at myself and said, "Hey, everyone, this is Sheri, and I'm about to take flight out of Fenton, Michigan!" I was smiling, eager to share it all. "It may not look like it now, but this hot air balloon is going to be ready to set sail in thirty minutes." I paused for effect. "I ain't scared."

I laughed for whoever was watching the video. But I wasn't kidding anyone. I was beyond scared.

Once the balloon had completely filled, it was time to board. I watched the men help the women step inside the wicker basket, and it swayed back and forth with the additional weight of each passenger. I had no idea that a hot air balloon ride was a hot Friday night date, and as the only single in the group, I suddenly felt a little uneasy. I wished I had waited to come along with a friend or one of the Dare Divas.

Sensing my unease, Mick offered his arm. "Come with me, young lady," he said, smiling broadly. I was likely twenty years his senior, and I couldn't help but smile at his charming demeanor and attempt to ease my discomfort. Though I could have easily boarded without assistance, I took his arm and stepped up into the basket.

Soon the basket bounced off the ground, and we began to ascend. Mick adjusted a lever, and the propane flame shot up the center of the balloon. I felt the heat like a furnace on my back. We floated by a majestic grove of oak trees seventy-five feet tall.

"Fall is a great time to go on a ride," Mick said. "Look over there. There aren't many opportunities to view eagles and their nests up close."

I looked where he was pointing, and right there, through some trees, I saw an eagle with its fledglings. I took out my cell phone to capture the amazing sight.

"This is our fourth hot air balloon ride," said Judy, an attractive brunette wearing tortoise-shell glasses. She and her husband, Paul, were both botanists. They entertained us with interesting facts about various plants and trees they had seen during previous rides.

"Every time, we see something we've never seen before," Judy said. "It's surprising. I mean, same company, pretty much the same flight route, but new things every time!"

"Takeoff and landing are what fascinate me," Mick said. "Even though we have an idea where we want to go, it's always a bit of a surprise where the wind will take us. Once we nearly got hooked to one of the trees!" He laughed. "Another time we landed near a herd of cows."

I was baffled by how Mick seemed completely at ease with the uncertainty of his job. I'm the opposite—persnickety about details and processes. Yet the *not knowing* was the very thing he most enjoyed.

As Mick continued recounting some of his unusual voyages, I felt another blast of heat from the propane. By this time, we were about halfway through our ride—too far from the launch site to return but still a long way from landing. With the fresh reminder from the flame, I thought about the damage the fire could do if it got out of control. A chill ran down my spine.

I began to ponder all the things that could go wrong and suddenly doubted my decision to go on this ride. I was, after all, two thousand feet in the air in a simple wicker basket held up by a fire-powered piece of fabric! I had no idea what I would do if the balloon caught fire or began plummeting toward earth. We had no parachutes, no ladder, not even buckets of water to put out flames.

"Hey, Sheri, can you take our pic?" Jeff said, breaking into my morbid thoughts. He extended his cell phone toward me.

I was gripping the thick rope handles inside the basket with both hands and willed myself not to faint. "One sec," I said, inhaling deeply.

Mick, likely trained to identify terrified riders, laid his hand on my shoulder. "You okay?" he asked. "Breathe." His calm presence pulled me out of the worst-case-scenario nightmare running through my mind.

I don't know why I panicked in that moment, but being on the balloon without a safety net felt a lot like my life in general. Even with my newfound boldness, fear had a way of creeping in and paralyzing me. It seemed that just when I thought I had figured things out, I could be surprised and knocked off my feet by the old, familiar fear.

"Wow," I said, shaking my head and looking at Mick. "I just had a moment, and my breath . . ." I struggled to explain the sudden panic I'd just experienced.

Marsha, a blonde woman in her sixties, clasped her hands. "Oh, goodie!" she exclaimed. We all looked at her curiously. "No, no," she said quickly. "I meant, I thought it was just me. I think I had a bit of a panic attack myself!"

Mick smiled. "It's perfectly normal—especially on a first ride—to put two and two together and start thinking of the worst. But in the eight years I've piloted this balloon, I haven't lost one yet." He winked at me and Marsha. "Much safer than riding in a car."

Pete, our captain, pointed out a large water tower that could hold over five hundred gallons and serviced the entire city of Fenton. He went over the history of the area, the mating pattern of loons, and the migration of indigenous birds. Soon I was listening and asking questions along with the others.

Just then the basket began to wobble as a violent gust of wind swept through. I quickly grasped the rope inside the balloon.

"Oh boy," I heard Judy shout as the balloon shook violently.
"What's going on? Are we okay?" Marsha shouted.

I held on tightly to the inner rope, buckling my knees. "Oh God, please." Mick's stats earlier had been given to calm us, but in that moment, the numbers meant nothing.

Both Mick and Pete adjusted some ropes and eased up on the force of the propane. As suddenly as it began, the turbulence stopped. But I wouldn't feel absolutely safe until we were on the ground and I was out of that wicker basket.

A few minutes later, I was surprised to hear Mick say, "Where should we land?"

Marsha laughed. "You're funny. There's a landing pad, right? Like where helicopters land?"

I turned so as not to see her reaction to the bad news coming her way. She clearly had not read the six-page waiver or heard Mick say earlier that he had no idea where we would land.

"Nope," Mick said cheerfully. "Nothing like that. We land where we can, and the vehicle following us comes and picks us up."

Despite Marsha's horror at this news, Pete and Mick started engaging the balloon in a smooth descent. Soon we hovered over a trilevel house with several acres surrounding it. Mick brought the balloon down with a slight bump in the center of the enormous backyard.

A woman ran over to the balloon from the porch of the house. "What a great birthday surprise!" she said, clapping her hands in delight. "Not for me but for my husband, Milt."

Milt, a bald gentleman with a thick gray beard, jogged over to us with a broad smile. As Mick opened the door of our vessel, Milt chivalrously offered us his arm. I grabbed this stranger's arm like he was my best friend. I was so relieved to be back on the ground safely.

"You guys looked great up there," Milt said. "I was hoping you'd touch down here. We've had it happen once before."

"But not on your birthday!" his wife exclaimed.

"Happy birthday!" each of us said.

Mick smiled and said, "As a gift, Balloon Quest gives you and your wife a ride in the future—on the house! Our compliments for letting us land on your property."

"We'll take you up on it," Milt said.

Our group of nine had bonded on the flight. Now we worked together, with instruction from the crew, to deflate the balloon, hand-roll it, and gather it in sections until it was laid flat. The crew then pulled it together and bunched it in place to load onto another vehicle while we got on a bus to head back to our cars.

My mission was complete, and I felt empowered to have done a dare on my own. The Divas may not have been with me physically, but I knew they were with me in spirit. My balloon journey never would have happened had we not concocted that first dare on the rapids in Virginia seven years earlier. The truth was, my friends had inspired me to spread my wings with this dare. They believed I was strong enough to venture out on my own.

The best of friends will inspire you, challenge you, and give you wings. In what ways has a friend sparked something new inside of you that you've wanted to explore?

●  ●  ●

A few days after my ride, Brenda and I compared notes. She had taken her ride the week before mine. "Girl," she said,

"I just kept smiling. I smiled so hard, I thought my mouth was going to freeze like that."

I laughed. I could picture that smile, even though we were talking on the phone.

I pressed my lips tight as a chill shot through me. It was the feeling of exhilaration I had after every dare. "It was so surreal, Bren," I said. "I kept thinking, 'I can't believe I'm doing this alone.' You know how scared I can get. But I was also glad I did it anyway, because the joy I felt is something that will be with me—be with us—for years to come."

"Yes!" Brenda said. "This one is our own special thing. Mia and Ang will have their things too."

"I was scared up there for a minute," I admitted.

"Me too," Brenda said quietly.

"The view was so cool," I said. "Like a more peaceful version of skydiving. The non-steroid version."

"Yep, no 'roids," Brenda joked. "I'd go skydiving again, though. We'll bring others, because everyone keeps telling me they really want to try it."

"The more the merrier," I said, though secretly I knew I was done with skydiving. "To future dares!"

"To future dares!" Brenda replied.

When we ended our call, I realized that while we'd both talked about being afraid, it had been only a small part of our conversation. Most of our talk centered on how exciting it had been to conquer yet another challenge. I wondered if my diminishing fear when it came to the dares was one expression of an overall change in my life.

Going on the hot air balloon ride on my own had been a big step for me. I sensed God calling me into something new—something on the horizon that I couldn't quite see.

Throughout my life, there have been times when I needed a precise word just for me, a clear indication, a direct voice from God on how to navigate the next big step. That was one of those times.

When I first lost Mannard, I was controlled by my fears and insecurities. I had depended on my husband and felt lost without him. But over time, I changed. I discovered that I was a capable person. I could make decisions and even strike out on my own. In the years that had passed since Mannard's death, I had sold a house, bought a new one, sent two kids off to college, and traveled halfway around the world—all by myself. In fact, the summer I took the hot air balloon ride was one of my most liberating years to date.

That year also provided sweet times when all I had was my own company—times jogging along a bike path with my favorite tunes in my earbuds, reading a beloved book on my comfy chair in my den, searching online for recipes to cook for friends and family, or having the remote control all to myself to binge on any indulgent, mindless cable show I wanted to without guilt.

At the same time, because people seemed to constantly be asking me if I would ever remarry, I had a growing awareness of my single status. But I wasn't lonely. God was upholding me, and I felt his presence each waking day. Every so often someone would ask if I was ready to get back out there, get back into the dating world. Things had changed considerably since I dated back in the eighties, with text messaging, online dating, and cyber safety concerns. I wasn't quite sure how to navigate this brave new frontier of dating.

The question for me was not only whether I'd date again but what my expectation was in a relationship. I'd married the man I longed for, he cherished me, and I adored him. And though we were not a perfect couple, nor did we have a flawless marriage, we had a resoundingly happy one. How would I top that? And should I even try?

I decided to give it a go. Mannard's mother, Joyce, wanted to introduce me to a widower, Michael Sherman, but at first I was reluctant.

"He's a good guy," she shared over the phone. "He had a great marriage, like you. His wife died from cancer. I really want you to talk to him."

Joyce and Michael were members of the same church, and she'd shared with him an article I wrote about widowhood following a speech he did at their church.

"He really identified with your article and just wants to chat to someone who has gone through what he has," she said.

I breathed heavily over the phone. "Ohhh, okay."

Mike called me two days later, we dated, and eighteen months later we were engaged. We married on July 13, 2019.

My mother-in-law matched me to both of my husbands—first her son, and now Michael. God indeed works in mysterious ways.

• • •

Not long before my balloon ride, I met with a woman of God I admired and who was active in ministry at her church.

"You're still so young, Sheri," she said over lunch. "Attractive, smart, independent . . . but you should know, you had a good one." She shook her head remorsefully as she buttered her bread. "My friend, you're not going to find another one like that."

I smiled, but I was a bit taken aback. Was this woman of God telling me my future was bleak—that my past was much better than what lay ahead?

"Whenever I would run into Mannard and talk about his service at church, he'd always find a way to bring the conversation back to you," she said. "I've never seen that type of devotion and earnest care from a husband—and let me tell you, I've counseled so many couples. It's rare. More rare than you can imagine."

I was pleased and delighted to hear her speak so fondly of Mannard. And while I know her words were not intended to wound me, they did make me question my future. Would I spend the rest of my life as a single woman? If so, what would that mean?

Though I knew this woman was a strong believer, I realized I still needed to question the veracity of her words. I had heard her preach at Bible studies and at conferences about the power of God. What he had done before, he could do again. Through God, my future could be better than my past, regardless of my circumstances.

After lunch, I hugged my friend, and we said goodbye. I was truly glad this meeting had occurred, because I had an incredible revelation. That very morning I had read the Bible and a devotional, and though that day's teaching said nothing about being a single woman in the kingdom of God, it talked about how Christ is the only one who can renew life and that every perfect gift comes from him.

God had given me a treasure when he gave me Mannard, but he could easily provide another loving husband if he chose to. I realized again the importance of reading and studying

God's Word. Only God can open my eyes to the truth and lead me on the right path.

Some of my single girlfriends were earnest, diligent, and steadfast in their beliefs of what an ideal mate would be. They had created an itemized list of traits that they desired in a spouse. Some of the qualities were physical: tall, lean, handsome; others were soul related: kind, patient, funny. Some of the qualities seemed to be more than any one human could muster, but I understood the women's deep-seated longing to be in a committed, loving relationship. I thought it was forthright to ask God for the desires of their hearts.

As a child who had been abandoned by her father, I never saw firsthand the love between a man and a woman. But at age eight, enveloped in the music at my grandmother's church, I was swept up in the emotion of the Holy Spirit and felt the love of Jesus—me, a little chocolate girl who didn't fully understand the concept of salvation. I still catch my breath at that small space of time when God touched me.

The pastor had been speaking about family, and how each member (the father and mother specifically) plays an instrumental part in the strength and fortitude of the family. I was thankful and relieved to have my mother and our family of two, but like my sweet friends who had a longing for an ideal mate, I had a heartfelt desire for a family. I don't recall all the pastor said, but I prayed my little-girl prayer, my secret talk between me and Jesus. While I didn't fully understand what marriage meant, I simply asked the Lord to bring me someone who would love me the way he wanted me to be loved. When I look back now, I believe God understood my request—that he would be the matchmaker and bring me the one he had made specifically for me. I would never need to worry or doubt God's gift.

The conclusion I came to about remarriage was that I could not fathom having any less of a love than I experienced with Mannard. I knew some people would never experience what Mannard and I had. Was I being unrealistic to think that lightning could strike again? I knew God could do anything, but most of all, I wanted him to align my heart to his plan—which for that season was embracing my singleness and the special relationship I shared with him.

Your heart may want one thing, but God may have a different plan for you. How do you reconcile your desires with God's plan as you move forward in happiness with your life?

. . .

Several years before Mannard died, Pastor Morman asked our church to participate in a corporate fast. For the entire month of February, we would pray and meditate, asking for clarity and understanding. We would eat like Daniel did when he arrived in Babylon and did not want to defile himself. Throughout our month of fasting, we would be on a strict vegan diet—no meat, no dairy, no eggs, no sodas, no chips, no coffee. *Oh, Lord.*

Fasting was a foreign practice to me. I remember talking to the Divas when the weight of the task hit us.

"No coffee?" Angenette asked in disbelief. "Well, I've fasted before and did without the java. I'll be strong. I can do it again."

I was glad I wasn't alone in wondering if the only things this practice would elicit were a grumpy spirit and a growling stomach. Ang was being positive, so maybe I could be too.

"God knows that I get hangry without meat," I said.

"It's not that bad," Mia said. "There are lots of really tasty vegan meals. We can eat whole wheat pasta with tomatoes and lots of sautéed veggies."

"And lots and lots of water," Brenda added. "Yum."

Angenette and I looked at each other, a single thought on our minds: if Brenda wasn't a sister in Christ, we might have smacked her.

"Hey, Whole Foods has these really good vegan cookies," Mia offered. "They have chocolate chip and oatmeal raisin. *Almost* as good as the real thing."

"Christian sustenance," Brenda said.

Ang turned to Brenda and leaned in. "You know what? You are really getting on my nerves!"

We laughed.

I was ready to put the plan into action: eat vegan and focus on Jesus. But when I arrived at Whole Foods, I was too late. There were six women in the aisle where the famous cookies had been on display. Despite my full cart of couscous, celery, and whole wheat pasta wheels, I had arrived too late for the cookies.

"Ma'am, I am so sorry," an employee said. "We had a good five cases of those cookies yesterday. We had to place a rush order for more today."

"Oh goodness, why?!" a woman standing nearby said. "I need those cookies. What happened? Did the whole church come and empty out the store?"

"CTab?" I said.

Her eyes widened. "You too?" We hugged in solidarity.

The Whole Foods employee then explained that they'd had enough cookies to last weeks, but our church fast had emptied their shelves in two days. "If your church had called us ahead of time, we could have arranged to bring more in."

I did finally get a box of those cookies from Mia, and after taking a bite, I understood their appeal.

CTab made the Daniel fast a yearly event, and as the years passed, I learned more about fasting and its benefits. Mannard and I actually began to look forward to that month. Not because either of us relished vegan cuisine, but because it humbled us to be reminded that there were some things we could never do on our own. If I wanted to know how to operate my life, the best way was to tune out my body and tune in to Christ.

• • •

Years later, after I left that lunch with my Christian friend, I decided I didn't want to wait for the annual church fast in February to seek God's will for my life. I decided to commit to fasting for the summer.

Fasting that summer opened my heart not only to what I wanted in my life but to what God wanted for me. I asked the Lord to help me see if my life plan was in alignment with his will. If not, I wanted Christ to change something inside of me so I could wholeheartedly lean into his will. I prayed that I would see his plan as a good one and that I would not be swayed or moved from it.

I also prayed that Jesus would make me happy and at peace with my singleness. I didn't ask him to bring me another good husband who would love me and take care of me. I had been learning to take care of myself and allowing God to heal me.

After Mannard died, I took a hard look at our finances and made adjustments. I honestly evaluated my weaknesses and flaws and tried to choose better, healthier ways of doing things. I took action steps to find joy even during times of angst and fear. And I discovered something beautiful: independence that occurred only because I gave up control of my life to Christ. I found that I was actually more than content in this new life. In a way, just me and my Father was pretty fabulous and felt wonderfully right.

I prayed that if God desired me to be single for the rest of my life, he would guide me as I continued down this road of fulfillment. If, instead, he desired to lead me back down the path of matrimony, I prayed I would be happy and have full peace about the man he selected for me.

When I ventured up in that hot air balloon, God revealed himself to me in a new way. The ride was beautiful and exhilarating, but I rose on my own, without my friends by my side. I enjoyed a dreamy sunset without a love of my own with whom to share it. Even though I was flying solo, that ride was a splendid, jubilant occasion. God had directed me to a place where I was happy and bubbling over with his love. And he would continue to do that regardless of whether I remained single or remarried one day.

Since Mannard's death, Jesus has become so dear to me. Through my quiet times with him and through the dares, he showed me what was possible when I sought him with all my heart. Just as Mick had guided us effortlessly through the wind and bumps of our hot air balloon ride, expertly using the fire to propel and not destroy, so God was using the fire of trials to make me stronger. I don't have to fear what life will bring, because God is always in control.

# 9

# dare to ascend

the mountain is taking me higher

APRIL 2014

When I returned home from my cruise, I met with the Dare
Divas to talk about our next dare. We were at Angenette's
house, sprawled out on her sofas like her comfy home was
our own.

"If you're looking for a really wild dare, I have one for
you," I said.

The Divas eyed me skeptically, waiting for whatever fun,
outlandish, but highly unlikely adventure I had in mind.

"Mount Kilimanjaro!" The words tumbled out in a rush.

I had first thought of hiking Mount Kilimanjaro when I
took my solo cruise through Africa and Asia. On that trip,
I met Absko, a twenty-five-year-old personal trainer who
had summited Mount Kilimanjaro. I remember thinking
that such a feat was for the young or superathletic—and at

forty-seven, I was neither. But the more I thought about it, the more I wanted the challenge.

Brenda and Ang stared at me, mouths agape.

"The dare of all dares." Mia jumped up from her seat, laughing and doing a funky dance.

I jumped up and joined her.

"You two are *crazy*," Ang said. She couldn't hide her true fun nature, though. She was dancing in her seat.

Mia danced over to her and pulled her up from the sofa.

"Yeah, pull me up," Ang said. "'Cause if I go on this dare, someone is gonna have to pull me up that mountain for sure."

I danced over to Brenda, and she smiled as I offered her my hand to join in the revelry. "Okay, okay," she said. "We can talk about it. Do you think we can do it? I mean, that's eight days of major physical exertion. *Eight days!*"

"We'll train for it, right?" Ang said. I could almost see the wheels turning in her mind. "We'll give ourselves a year to whip our bodies into shape. We can research all the good hiking websites and get tips from those who have gone before us."

Our excitement grew as the four of us talked about making this dream dare a reality.

"That mountain ain't got nothing on us," Ang said confidently. "It's all a mental game."

## SEPTEMBER 2018

Four years had passed since our conversation in Ang's living room, and six years since Mannard died. Now here we were in Tanzania, at the base of Mount Kilimanjaro. Each year thirty thousand people from around the world attempt to summit Uhuru Peak, and this year we were among them! As we set off on our adventure, our climbing guides and crew sang a boisterous song in Swahili. They danced as if they were at a wedding celebration instead of about to climb a formidable mountain.

"*Wageni, mwakaribishwa!*" (Guests, you are welcome!)

"*Kilimanjaro, hakuna matata!*" (Kilimanjaro, there is no problem!)

I found myself dancing to the beat. The concerns I'd had about the challenging climb ahead melted away as I danced along, caught up in the jubilance.

"*Jambo, jambo, bwana.*" (Hello, hello, sir.)

"*Habari gani.*" (How are you?)

"*Mzuri sana.*" (Very fine.)

I felt my courage rise as the guides sang. Maybe the climb wouldn't be as difficult as I'd imagined. The Tanzanian men, who were in their twenties, wore long-sleeve shirts and fleece jackets. The temperature was 55 degrees. A bit chilly, but I was warmed and energized by the preclimb dance party. The other Divas joined me in spinning and shimmying at the start of the climb.

I tried to mimic the rhythmic up-and-down sway of the Africans' arms and legs, but it looked like I was stomping grapes. "Am I doing this right?" I asked a guide, who was sporting a University of Michigan jersey. I smiled at the reminder of my alma mater, a piece of home right here in Africa.

He smiled back and answered in a thick Tanzanian accent, "You can do no wrong dance here. Moving your body to the music any way you want is a good thing."

I turned to see the Divas getting in on the excitement. Mia swung her hips to the beat. Ang's long braids swayed as she bent over and shimmied her shoulders like she was dancing at home in front of a mirror instead of on display. Brenda danced with a megawatt smile that lit up the place. I thought about all we had been through together and felt a deep sense of gratitude for these women. Without their love and encouragement, I wasn't sure where I'd be.

Our hike began uneventfully. Our group was made up of the four Dare Divas and six others. Wayne was our section leader, and Steve was the commander over the crew. As we began winding slowly up the lower part of the mountain, twenty or so young men passed us, carrying large bags that held food, tents, sleeping bags, extra clothes and shoes, rain and snow gear, and emergency supplies. Each individual sack easily weighed a good thirty to forty pounds. But the young men carried them effortlessly on their heads. I was in awe of their physical ability. As they disappeared on the trail up ahead, we continued to climb.

"Glad one of my training routines at home was a series of squats," I said. "Putting those to use already. Oh joy."

"I feel like I should have trained for a marathon," Brenda groaned. We walked over rough, rocky terrain in a single-file line behind Wayne. "Those hikes at home seem like kiddie walks compared to this," she continued.

During the previous year, Brenda and I had been training buddies. Two times a week, I had packed my bags with ten-pound weights and hiked through metropolitan parks for six to eight hours. Brenda did long hikes once a week and then twice a week a couple of months before the hike.

Suddenly Mia stopped in her tracks, and I bumped into her. "What's that?" she asked, an expression of shock and horror on her face.

She had not heeded Wayne's warning not to look up. I also looked up and saw what appeared to be a line of ants marching up a path that wound up and up before disappearing into the clouds.

Brenda gasped. "Where's the top?"

We all stood there with our mouths hanging open.

"There is no top," Angenette answered from behind. "Not for a long, long, long time. What have you gotten us into, Sheri?" She pointed her hiking stick at me. It was the one I had given her as a wedding gift the year before.

I gritted my teeth. "Was this dare my suggestion?" I asked innocently. I shortened my step so we could walk side by side.

"You know doggone well it was you!" she said, shoving my shoulder playfully.

I smiled and shook my head. "Why did you guys listen to me? Of all the dares? Why didn't y'all say, 'Crazy lady, no! We ain't doing that!'"

"Come now," Wayne said sternly. "No talking. *Pole, pole.*" We would hear these words over and over again on our journey. "Slow, slow," he said, interpreting the phrase. "We say here in our country, 'Little by little, a little becomes a lot.' No rush."

"Oh, don't worry," Ang quipped. "Ain't nobody rushing."

We all laughed.

Four hours into the climb, I was feeling tapped out. I had known the climb would be difficult, but I was surprised by how quickly my energy began to fade as we trudged up the steep incline. The literature on the scenic Lemosho Route had mentioned rain forests, tall grasses, and lichen-covered volcanic rock. So I was shocked when after just one hour we began a steep climb upward, navigating giant boulders.

My quadriceps and adductor muscles burned from the repetitive series of deep lunges we did to scale the boulders. The motion was similar to the one I'd done at the gym in preparation for the climb. But instead of doing three sets of fifteen, I had just done at least two hundred in a row—and we still had four hours to go.

"The pamphlets said this was a hike," I said, laughing as I took a seat on a rock during one of our breaks. "Not true! This thing here—it's straight up *American Ninja Warrior*!"

"That's the truth, girl." Brenda was sitting on an adjacent rock. "I trained hard! I *thought* I trained hard." She laughed. "I hiked miles with all that weight, but I needed to do more. Like acrobat training."

I laughed. "And the altitude! I could breathe when I was training in Michigan. Not on this mountain. The air's so thin up here."

Back on the path, we came to a steep rock ledge we would need assistance to scale. I extended my arms high above my head so Wayne and another guide could pull me up. Their strength and endurance amazed me. They had taken this route hundreds of times before—to them it was routine. But with this steep incline so early in the hike, I was beginning to wonder if we'd bitten off more than we could chew with this dare.

• • •

If you're like me, when you've moved forward with an idea or feat, you may have second-guessed yourself in the midst of it. My climb up Mount Kilimanjaro was not the first time I felt I had gotten myself in a pickle physically and called on the Lord to get me through. When I was thirty, I took up running to lose the thirty pounds of stubborn baby weight that hung on after Danielle was born. After six months of running five days a week, the extra weight was gone, but more had changed than just my figure. I had suddenly morphed into a committed runner who looked forward to the daily burn.

The members of the running group I'd joined were seasoned racers. One day I overheard them talking about running the Detroit Free Press Marathon. *I could do that*, I thought.

"Marathon? You've never even run a 10k!" Mannard exclaimed. I had just told him my crazy idea as we drove to the movie theater for date night. "Girl, you haven't even run a 5k! Seriously? What makes you think you can run twenty-six miles?"

"Twenty-six point two," I corrected him. "And you forget. I run five miles practically every day, and a 5k is only 3.1 miles."

"Yeah, but that's not *racing*," he said. "Racing and trotting down the street aren't the same thing."

"I don't trot!" I smirked. "So are you gonna support me or what?"

Mannard gripped the steering wheel with both hands—something he did when he was contemplating what to say next. "I will," he began slowly. "But you'll need to get both of our moms to help with the kids. You'll need to do some serious training for that, and it will take a lot of time."

He was right. With my full-time job, two toddlers, and a house to maintain, I needed the help of both our moms to even attempt it. Lucky for me, they gladly volunteered.

On the day of the race, I wore a garbage bag over my running clothes to ward off the thirty-degree chill of the early morning.

Mannard rubbed my arms to warm them as I waited for the race to begin. "You're gonna be all right. You're gonna be all right," he said—I think more to reassure himself than me.

I felt ready. As part of my six-month training schedule, I had run up to fifty miles per week and participated in a ten-mile run and even a twenty-two-mile race two weeks earlier. The "wall"—that point of exhaustion where I felt like puking and throwing in the towel—always came at mile 13.

On race day, I made an unfortunate mistake. I changed my routine, which is a no-no. I wore a brand-new sports bra. As I ran, it began digging into my shoulder blades. I would have torn off the horrible thing, but I didn't want to flash other racers.

A runner from my group handed me a cup at a water stop. "Just keep going!" he said. "Take a swig and let's roll."

At the halfway point, I was bone weary and didn't have anything in me. I longed to just lie down on the side of the road. My pace was pathetic as I jog/walked a twenty-minute mile. Speed walkers passed me by, some juggling balls and dribbling basketballs. I was humiliated.

But I kept going. At times I barely walked. Other times I stopped altogether to catch my breath. At mile twenty-six I had a mere 0.2 miles to go, but I felt every foot of it. The final push was excruciating. I crossed the finish line with a time of 5:27:08.

Mannard was waiting for me. He scooped me up like a sack of potatoes and hoisted me in the air. "You did it!" he cheered. "Dang! I can't believe you did it!" He planted a big smooch right on my lips.

In the end, I had lacerations from the faulty athletic gear and felt as if I had been dragged through the streets. To be honest, I was just glad it was over. But I felt proud of my accomplishment, and I was glad that Mannard was proud of me too.

. . .

I thought back to that marathon as we closed in on six hours of climbing that first day. I still felt strong, but I was also hitting a wall. This level of energy output was foreign to me. But my mind was alert, and I just kept my poles clacking on the ground, *pole* style.

"We'll be at camp soon," Wayne said. "Then you can put your feet up, eat, and rest." I glimpsed a flag waving in the distance. Day one was coming to an end.

When the Divas and I arrived at camp, we were tired, but we jumped up and down in elation. We circled up and embraced like we had done at the end of so many dares and took a celebration photo at the day one marker.

The crew who had run ahead had already pitched our tents and placed sleeping bags, clothes, and essentials inside. After placing our daypacks in the tents, we gathered in a large outdoor tent to eat and receive a briefing on the next seven days. We feasted on a delicious meal of cucumber soup, white rice, bananas, boiled chicken, toast, and ginger tea.

After dinner, Steve and Wayne briefed us on the itinerary for the next day.

"Tomorrow we wake early," Steve said. "I'll bring hot tea to your tents at 7:00. Breakfast will be at 8:00. At 9:00 we set off for eight or so hours, depending on your speed." He had escorted hundreds of hikers up the mountain and had supreme endurance. He could climb while hauling daypacks and his own equipment. "Don't forget to take your altitude sickness medication," he continued. "Very important. Take it seriously."

"Diamox doesn't agree with me," Ang said, sipping her ginger tea. "Been taking other alternatives—beet juice, ginger."

"I'll keep an eye on you," Steve said, looking at her with concern. "That beet juice will make you do things. Things that make you go, go, go!"

"Oh no, Ang!" Mia said, catching his meaning.

I cringed at the thought of being on the mountain, needing to "go, go, go" and having no bathroom.

"I have no choice," Ang said. "I never had that experience with having to 'go, go, go.' It's been great for me—no negative effect. I can't take the meds, and I brought the beet juice powder because it's been a big help. I tried it when I visited Machu Picchu, and the headaches and dizziness were terrible. I'll take my chances with the beet juice.. Either way, it won't be pleasant. But I'll just give it my best."

"That's all we can do," I said, patting her on the back.

．．．

After a sleepless night with the wind whipping the outside of my tent, my sense of humor seemed to have disappeared with my energy. I ate a breakfast of porridge, boiled egg, and stale bread. Though it was far from appetizing, I was hungry, and I eagerly gobbled it down with my ginger tea. I was in no position to be picky. I needed the nourishment.

The second day progressed much like the first, except each of us was more fatigued.

Mia stayed right behind Wayne, not wanting to fall behind. I picked up my pace to walk next to her.

"How's it going?" I asked.

Mia had been ill the week before we left the States. The Divas had provided her with cold medicine and remedies they'd brought along, but nothing had helped.

"I can't believe I still have a sore throat," she said. "And my head is pounding."

"Are the meds helping at all?"

"A little," she said. "I'm feeling better than I was two days ago. Of all the times to get sick. Ugh."

I recalled what we'd learned as we researched how to have a successful climb. According to hikers who had summited, the secret to success was not to rush it, to not attempt speeding to the finish. Marathoners and extreme athletes who had completed Ironman competitions had tried to do just that, only to be worn down by altitude sickness and harsh conditions. Going too fast could be hazardous, our guides warned. *Pole, pole*—slow, slow—was the key to success on this mountain.

I thought about how this was also true of my life following Mannard's sudden passing. I hadn't been able to rush the grief, the healing, the acceptance of life without him. But slowly, as I pushed myself to do exciting dares with my friends, I began to see that God was present in my life in bigger ways than I had imagined. He was with me in every slow step.

As I hiked, my thoughts turned to my son and daughter. I wished they could see me powering through, climbing this mountain. They had adored and respected their father, but I hoped I inspired them too. I hoped they saw me as an example of someone who persevered—someone who glorified the Lord through the hardships and embraced the wonderful life he had given me.

As they began their own careers in finance and marketing, my greatest wish was that they would live their own daring lives and understand that when a shocking event occurs—and it will—moving forward is achievable. It takes time and work, but it is possible with perseverance and trust in the Lord.

When you are pushing toward fulfilling a goal, don't be surprised if your family is silently taking it all in, watching in awe as you navigate your life. What are some things you say to your loved ones to encourage them to go after their dreams?

• • •

The next few days blurred together as we made steady, slow progress up the mountain. Each of us was exhausted and dealing with our own ailments. Mia's cold seemed to be getting worse. Ang fought altitude sickness. I pushed through searing pain in my heel from plantar fasciitis. Even Brenda was losing steam. None of us had been sleeping well, and all of us were sore.

On day five, our exhaustion seemed to reach its peak. The terrain was getting more challenging. We had to leapfrog over slippery boulders that lay near drop-offs. I was thankful to be following experienced guides.

Our guides were everything we needed and more. They were patient, and their expertise shined. They were able to detect when we needed to rest and say comforting and reassuring words when we needed it most. And yes, they were stern when it came to our safety.

We waited in line to navigate a particularly tricky rock formation that loomed in the air some fifty feet above us.

It reminded me of a man-made climbing wall you'd see inside a sporting goods store. After navigating the climb to the top, Angenette used one hand to grip the rock and the other to reach for Wayne and make a lateral leap to a neighboring boulder. Steve stayed just behind her in case she began to fall.

"Here, grab my hand," Steve said to Angenette.

Angenette was focused; sweat beaded on her forehead. After she made the leap, she said, "*That* was not in the brochure. *That* was not hiking. That was a death-defying Jedi move!"

We all hooted. It was indeed mind-blasting.

"Sit over there! No time," Steve chided. "This will pass and we will be on our way. Now, Brenda, come, come."

Brenda complied and, like Angenette, hurled her body across to the other boulder. Mia and I did the same. Our stress was at an all-time high. No one verbally blamed me for coming up with this foolhardy idea that was pushing us to our limits, but in that moment, I kicked myself for it.

Our climb seemed to go on and on that day. Our normal five- to ten-minute breaks were no longer cutting it. Our fatigue coupled with lack of sleep was prompting all-out anarchy in our ranks.

"Are we almost there?" I said in the whiny voice of a five-year-old. "You said forty minutes ago that we were almost there."

Steve quickened his step. "I did say that, but you're walking slower and the breaks are becoming longer. The trail usually takes eight hours, but it's now nine." He paused. "You will get there, but the point is to get there in one piece. You don't want to get injured. So keep pushing. *Pole, pole.*"

"This is unreal," Ang complained. "Someone carry my backpack, please." She handed hers over to a crew member.

"Me too," Mia said. "If I have to crawl to camp, I will. But not with this pack on my back."

At hour eleven of what was supposed to be an eight-hour hike, all of us were beginning to shut down. Ang took shallow breaths. Mia walked with a limp. Brenda was unusually quiet. Darkness was falling, and with my headlight in the gear up ahead at camp, I began to panic.

Brenda must have been feeling the same thing. "I'm starting to lose it," she said. She had been our rock, so when she articulated her feelings, I gave in to my frustration.

"That's it! I. Have. Had. It. *When* will we get there? Don't play with me, Steve!" I said, using the calmest voice I could muster in that moment.

"Calm, calm," he said, patting my back. "We are about one hour from—"

"An hour?!" Mia yelped.

"Please, God, no!" Brenda cried.

"Where's the beet juice?" Ang said as she reached for her own supply in her bag. "I need something." Though Ang did not have any difficulty breathing, her blood oxygen saturation levels were getting low.

Steve rushed over to help Ang, and we took yet another break.

Though we were reaching our breaking point, our situation clearly didn't faze Steve and the crew. They had ample experience with the mountain. They knew exactly what we would encounter because they had mastered the mountain. They didn't focus on time the way we did. They weren't caught up in surviving the climb; their minds were already at camp.

When I was in the midst of my grief after Mannard's death, I had a hard time keeping my eyes on the destination—the goal of glorifying God through my time on earth. But even when I lost sight of that, my faithful guide was still with me. He saw that I had no idea how to help my teenagers start a new school year without their dad. He saw that my finances were falling apart and that I couldn't fix a mortgage that was underwater. He saw that I was uncertain about my ability to lead our family when I had never done it before. At the time, I felt as if I was drowning in my problems, and I could see no way for everything to turn out all right. But even then, God saw me and was guiding me.

*My child*, he whispered, *focus on where you're going—the end game. Delight in me, put in the effort, and I will get you there.* I didn't hear those words in my spirit until months after being in the midst of grief, but when I did, I knew they had been true all along. Yet the path to take wasn't always clear to me. Obstacles seemed to greet me at each bend in the road. Even in the months leading up to the climb, I experienced uncertainty about what my future held. My dream job of being a writer seemed to be slipping away. Attaining my goal was taking much longer than I anticipated, and I wondered if it would ever happen. But through the Word and his Spirit, God was continually reminding me of who he created me to be and that he was in control of my destiny.

. . .

We finally reached camp after dark, twelve hours after we began. I didn't pester the girls to pose for a commemorative photo. I didn't go to the food tent either. I was more tired than hungry and simply couldn't stomach another round of ginger tea, rice, and cucumber soup. I'd try to choke down some porridge and peanut butter on stale bread in the morning. At that moment, all I wanted to do was to hunker down in four layers of clothes inside my minus-ten-degree sleeping bag and try to sleep as the wind whipped against my tent.

I had just untied my hiking boots when Steve asked to unzip my tent.

"Sheri, are you there? Are you dressed?"

"Yes, I'm here. What's up?"

Steve ducked into the tent. "I brought you food."

My stomach turned, and I cringed at my ungratefulness. There were people on this very continent and back at home who were starving and would have been grateful for my food.

"That was nice of you, but I'll pass," I said wearily. Steve didn't give up. He left a steaming-hot bowl of food we hadn't had before—mashed potatoes and boiled chicken with tomato sauce. I quickly devoured the whole thing.

After dinner, I snuggled into my sleeping bag and closed my eyes. I hoped that exhaustion and a full stomach would add up to a deep and sound sleep. But three hours later, at midnight, I was wide awake and aware of every sound around me. I heard tents unzip and the crunch of the rocky soil as others trudged to the porta potties. I heard the snores of other campers. And I heard what sounded like the screeches of prehistoric creatures. Steve later informed me the chilling sounds were only monkeys communicating with each other.

The next morning, day six, we entered the food tent wearing our full gear—winter jackets and snow pants along with other assorted cold-weather gear. Overnight, the temperature had dropped to twenty-five degrees.

Everything on the table looked unappealing. I forced myself to nibble on a hard-boiled egg.

"Tonight we summit," Mia said, bundled in multiple layers. Her plate consisted of scrambled eggs with a side of cold meds.

"Finally!" I said. "I don't know how much longer I can do this."

Brenda breathed deeply. "I want . . . I want . . ." She sat next to me in a folding chair.

I picked up the ginger tea and began to pour it in her cup. Like the rest of us, she was fed up with the stuff but needed the hydration and added benefit of it. The nourishment the guides, staff, and cooks provided for us was plentiful and gave us the sustenance that was so needed. But our irritation due to exhaustion and desiring those comfort meals from home was getting the best of us.

Brenda pushed my hand away. "No, not that." She sniffled. "I want my *husband*. I want I.D."

I reached over and grasped her hand.

Ang suddenly welled up. "I'm just exhausted. So I probably won't be able to summit."

"What? We won't be able to take our Dare Diva picture together?" After the words left my mouth, I realized how insensitive they sounded. So often the dares had been about the great picture at the end, but today, on this journey, our health issues would prevent the perfect snap.

Ang shook her head, and a tear fell from her eye.

I was shocked. Ang never cried. This was real. Despite the fact that I believed we were in capable hands with Wayne and Steve, this was the first time I felt like the dare might be too much for us to handle.

"Ang," I said, "it's not about finishing. Look, we have lots to be thankful for! Just trying, just coming this far, is way cool."

"Yeah, Ang," Mia said. "I'm proud of all of us."

Because of the previous day's extra-long journey, Steve wanted us ready to head out at 7:00 a.m. sharp so we could reach camp, rest, and then climb at midnight to the summit.

When Brenda and I arrived late from packing up our gear in our tents, Angenette snapped, "If you're gonna be late, tell somebody you need assistance before our takeoff time."

"We are trying our best," Brenda said. "And we did ask for help. I'm usually timely, but I'm not sleeping."

"None of us are sleeping, Bren."

"I don't need *you* to tell *me* what I already know!" Brenda said in a way that was uncharacteristic for her. "We will get there, so stop. Just stop."

I thought about interrupting and telling my friends it was all going to be okay, but I just focused on the ground in front of me. I didn't think I could bear a fight. I didn't have the energy in me to be a peacemaker.

As we trudged up the path, I prayed for each of my friends. I prayed for our good health and safety. Although I felt safe with Wayne and Steve, I knew there were risks. Each day we had seen a helicopter flying in to pick up a hiker who needed medical attention. On day six, we saw five helicopters. The increase in air traffic was an indication of the increased danger as people had to be taken off the mountain.

Six hours in we finally reached twelve thousand feet above sea level—higher than any of us had ever been. The air was thinner and the clouds were so close it felt like we could grasp them and tuck the mist in a bottle.

That evening was unlike anything we had experienced on the mountain. High-speed winds whipped at our tents, making it feel like we were inside a hurricane. *Surely they will cancel the summit*, I thought. *It has to be too risky to have anyone up there. What's the chance that someone could be blown away to her death?*

At 11:30 p.m., Steve had still not canceled the hike. I trudged to the mess tent to eat what would be my last breakfast on the mountain before we descended. This was *the* night of nights. We would depart at midnight and hike for six hours to the summit. At the top, we would greet the dawn and be rewarded by a sunrise. Then we would hike six hours back down to base camp and spend three additional days descending to the bottom of the mountain.

Angenette was settled in her tent, the beet juice having helped immensely. Steve was diligent to check her levels and warned her that if they did not improve, he would guide her down the mountain. Thankfully, that wasn't needed. She was still able to breathe without an oxygen mask, but she was bone tired. She would stay at camp while we attempted the summit.

"I hope Ang will be okay," Brenda said as we ate breakfast. "I'm going to give it my all, but I'm exhausted."

"I'm going to go as far as I can," Mia said. In the last day, her cold had subsided, but she was still not at her best.

"That's all we can do at this point," I said, forcing down what I hoped would be my last sip of ginger tea.

During the first few hours of our night hike, we walked over jagged limestone. In my ski gear, each step felt heavy. My body felt weak, and the wind pushed against me, causing even greater fatigue.

After three hours, the Dare Divas were tapped out.

"I'm bowing out," Mia said, leaning on Wayne like he was a wooden post. "I'm going back down to camp."

"Why not go just a little farther?" Brenda said.

"It's more than a little farther," Mia yelled through the wind. "It's at least another four hours to the summit. I've already done three, and I don't want anyone trying to convince me to keep going right now."

We could see Mia was spent, so we allowed her to turn around. Steve guided her back down to base camp while Brenda and I continued on.

An hour later, the limited resources in my physical body and my mental toughness were both depleted. I felt a weariness I had never encountered in my fifty-one years.

Steve, the superhuman guide, had somehow managed to catch back up with us. What was a six-hour journey for most, he could hike/run in a third of the time.

"Mia?" I asked when I saw him.

"Back at camp," he said.

"I'm so tired. How much longer?"

Steve looked at me, and I saw the first sign of annoyance in his eyes. "So?" he said. "And? You're tired. What does that matter? Can you breathe? Looks like yes!"

I felt a deep sense of shame that my body was failing me—that with all my talk of climbing every mountain, both physically and spiritually, I wouldn't summit that day. I shook my head. "I can't, Steve."

After so much preparation and planning, I was disappointed that I wasn't going to complete the dare the way we had planned by summiting. But the reality is that sometimes God says no. He said no when I prayed for a miracle the morning Mannard died. When the ambulance arrived and the EMTs began to work on Mannard, I prayed that they would resuscitate him, that there would be a Lazarus moment—that my beloved would breathe once again and our happy life together would continue on. The Lord did not ignore me. He answered my prayer, but the answer was, "No, not this time, Sheri."

Once again I felt the sting of disappointment and sadness and had to will myself to accept the Lord's answer. I had to trust that his no was for my highest good. There would be other times when he would say yes, but this wasn't one of them.

Brenda outlasted us all. In the end, she didn't summit either, but she got pretty darn close. Two hours after sunrise, when the strong wind had not died down, she was forced to turn back. While at the Meru area, she waved her University of Michigan flag, waved our Dare Diva flag, and snapped a picture for us all.

• • •

Back at camp, the four of us gathered together by our tents. We posed in triumph, smiling brightly and holding the Dare Diva flags Mia had created.

"No regrets?" I asked as we huddled in a circle, blocking the wind.

"Well, I'm glad I did it. Mostly I appreciate the time we all bonded more than the hike. I'm still trying to reconcile all of this," Ang said.

Mia placed an arm around her shoulders. "Agreed! I can barely walk, but on the bright side, I've probably lost some pounds! I honestly wish we had gone all the way, but this has been the best dare of all."

"God brought us here, and he had us go as far as he wanted us to go," Brenda said. "If it's okay with him, it's okay with me."

For me, the best part of climbing Mount Kilimanjaro was when it was over. I was not like some of the die-hard climbers who passed me along the trail. For them, Mount Kilimanjaro was just another summit to conquer. They had already mastered hiking at high altitude, and the pain and exhaustion were just part of the experience.

But that was not me—one time was plenty. Mount "Killa" was my Goliath. My time there had revealed both my weakness and my strength. The day that I gazed up the mountain and saw hikers who looked like ants disappearing into the clouds, I wanted to give up. But I remembered the words of Psalm 121:1–2: "I lift up my eyes to the hills. From where does my help come? My help comes from the LORD, who made heaven and earth" (ESV).

The visual of a mountain is so powerful. It stands strong and firm when chaos swirls around it. When Mannard died, chaos threatened to win. But God was my help. My mountain. As I looked to him, I realized that he was always with me. The Creator of heaven and earth, of Mannard and me, cared about me and would help me.

Even though I was not able to summit, my perspective had changed. I realized that God had brought me to exactly where he wanted me and not a step farther. The blessing was in having the faith to attempt something difficult—"the dare of all dares"—and watching God sustain me through it. I had climbed higher than I ever had before, and I was grateful. I knew where my help came from, and I would keep my eyes on him.

# 10

# dare to be wild

### fortified for my best life

**SEPTEMBER 2018**

Two days after our grueling trek up Kilimanjaro, the Divas and I set out on a three-day safari through Lake Manyara National Park, the Ngorongoro Crater, and Tarangire Park in Tanzania. *What a difference a day makes*, I thought. One day I was struggling and using every last ounce of energy to descend the mountain after an eight-day hike, and the next, I was riding in style, snapping photos of animals.

After being in tents, sweaty and filthy for eight days, the four of us were overjoyed to have hot water, plumbing, and comfortable accommodations. We looked forward to a couple of days of relaxation with our safari driver escorting us through the wilderness.

With our neat cornrows, faux locs, box braids, and twists, the African people may have thought we were born in Tanzania—until we opened our mouths. We'd received the styles in the US before we left so that our hair would be easy to care for during our African adventure.

Nato, our driver and safari guide, stretched his arms wide and beamed with pride. "This is nature's home, yes?" he said, flashing us a blindingly white smile. "There are more than five hundred species of birds here. We have hippos, wild dogs, leopards, rhinos! Everything you can see at the zoo, only up close and uncaged."

"Amazing," I said. "And no threat of poachers?"

"Yes, some," Nato said. "But we are very watchful. Everywhere—here, other reservations, protected lands—there are targets on these animals' backs. Wherever there are predators or men, they are targets."

The Divas and I were entranced by his dialect and passion for his homeland.

"Only, these animals are not like us," he continued. "They don't worry themselves to death about enemy until enemy make himself plain. They just live."

*They just live.*

• • •

Even before we married, Mannard showed me he knew how to live well. One day, four months into our dating relationship, he called me to say we were going to have a picnic.

"Really?" I asked, watching the pouring rain outside my window. "Not this weekend, right?"

Mannard chuckled. "It's sunny over here at my house," he said. "No clouds or rain in sight."

The forecast predicted heavy precipitation for the entire Detroit area for the following three days. "Okay," I said. "So a torrential rain cloud is over the whole state but dodged you, huh?"

"Yep," he said. "You'll see. Pick you up in an hour."

When I opened the front door an hour later, Mannard stood there holding a gigantic umbrella. He escorted me to the passenger side of his car, retracted the umbrella, and raced around the car to climb in.

"Are we going to Arizona or California?" I asked playfully as rain pounded on the windshield. "'Cause you'd have to be a magician to wish away all this."

"Nope. You'll see."

I watched his handsome profile, wondering what he was up to.

Ten minutes later we drove up to his home and pulled into the driveway. I didn't say a word as he retrieved the umbrella and accompanied me up the walkway. He unlocked the front door and swung it open.

I caught my breath. Inside the small but tidy living room, Mannard had spread an ornate patchwork quilt across the green carpet. A tan wicker basket and blue plastic plates lay on top of the quilt, along with napkins and clear tumblers. Red, blue, and purple pillows lay scattered around the quilt.

Mannard grinned at me as we removed our shoes. "Not Arizona," he said, "but at least it's dry. Mom is out for a while, and I thought we'd pretend we're in a warm location."

"My heart is warm," I said, gently kissing his cheek and kneeling before the splendor.

Mannard retrieved four sandwiches wrapped in waxed paper and spread them out before me. "Wasn't sure what kind of sandwich you'd like. Mom said I should offer some options. There's turkey, ham, roast beef, and tuna. I was the chef."

"Yum." I chose the turkey sandwich and added chips and a pickle to my plate. Mannard opened a liter of Faygo orange soda. His favorite band, Earth, Wind & Fire, played on the tape player, and the lyrics to their hit song "Fantasy" took me away.

Mannard handed me a slightly wilted pink carnation. I sniffed the modest flower and emotion overwhelmed me. I was bowled over by his kindness. Where did this man come from?

My father had abandoned me at birth. And while I knew the men in my life—my uncles and cousins—cared for me, no one had ever gone out of his way to make me feel adored. Mannard's sweet gesture was the most heartwarming thing a man had ever done for me.

"We can go to a movie or watch one here," Mannard said, clearly not sure how to read my response to his grand gesture.

"This, this . . ." I tried to put into words what I was feeling. "This is the most beautiful thing ever, Mannard. Seriously."

Mannard looked down. "Well, it's not dinner at a five-star restaurant or anything . . ."

I reached for his hand. "This is better than any five, six, or ten-star restaurant. I can't believe you thought of it. It's just . . . really kind. I love it. I love it all." I stopped short of telling him I loved him, even though it was true. I didn't want to spoil the moment with an "I love you; do you love me?" conversation so early in our relationship. That would happen two weeks later when he was the first to utter the words.

"You know, it wasn't a lot of effort. And I will take you somewhere really nice too. But I just thought we'd enjoy this. The event doesn't have to be fancy with us."

On the grayest of days, sunshine surrounded us in that moment as the music played on.

The Lord had always been my provider—*the* provider. He had brought Mannard to me, just for me. He had un-leashed his grace on me, filling the holes and places of lack with his love.

When my children ask me when I knew I loved their father, I tell them it was the day their dad brought sunshine on a rainy day with a picnic lunch in his living room.

Twenty-seven years later, when Mannard passed away, it felt like that sunshine had been replaced by eternal gloom. A few days before the funeral, I talked with my kids about how they wanted to honor their father's life.

"I can't let Dad go without saying something," Danielle said softly. "Maybe I should write a letter. I hate that I didn't have the chance to say goodbye."

The three of us were in my bedroom, sprawled on the bed like when they were five and six—only now they were sixteen and seventeen.

"I know," David said. He stared at the ceiling with his head on my pillow. "I could write a novel. I just wish I had more time."

I was lying on my side, pushing my fingers through Dani-elle's thick tresses. I hoped the ritual was as soothing to her as it was to me. "Write it down," I said. "Or type it on your phone. It doesn't have to be long. If you feel okay about it, you can say it at his home-going."

"Why do they call it that, Mom?" Danielle asked. "A home-going?"

David scoffed. "Yeah, why? That's stupid! It's not home. Home is where we are. That's what you and Dad always said."

I recognized that this could be a teachable moment, a "Jesus moment," but Jesus seemed so far away. "Yes, I said that," I began. "Here on earth, wherever we're together, is home. When our bodies leave here, our souls go to our heavenly home, and one day we'll be together again."

They remained silent. I wasn't sure if they were absorbing the truth or simply not wanting to debate it with their grieving mother.

At the funeral, more than two hundred people attended to pay their respects and say farewell. Many came up to me to personally express what Mannard meant to them.

Before us, Mannard was laid out in repose, one hand cupped unnaturally over the other. He was lifeless but still strangely looked like himself, maybe because of the eyeglasses I'd affixed to his nose at the family viewing. He was dressed in a navy suit that I thought was becoming on him and he had favored. I leaned down to kiss his forehead as my kids stood on each side of me, seeing his earthly body for the last time. I cried streams of tears as I said goodbye to my beloved.

David coaxed me away from the coffin. "Mom, we have to address everyone." He escorted Danielle and me up to the podium.

I was about to step forward and speak on behalf of our family, when David stepped up and commanded the microphone.

"My family and I would like to thank you for attending today," he said. "It means the world to us. We will never forget your kindness. We each want to share a bit about our father." He pulled out his phone to read the words he'd prepared. "My name is David Mannard Hunter. I have my father's name, and I hope and pray I can always live up to what that name means. To live up to who my dad was, a man of integrity who served the Lord and cherished and loved his family. He was a hard worker and cared about people, and he expected no less of me and my sister."

As David spoke, I was stunned by the clear, concise way he was describing his father's character. I felt proud to be his mother.

"I can go on and on about my father," David said. "In essence, I know what it means to be a man, because I saw it every day in how my father lived. He was gentle, patient, and strong. He used his words very carefully to uplift people. He was a provider who took his role of parenting and leading our family seriously. I will be forever grateful to my father. I love you, Dad, and I'll do my best to make you proud."

When David finished, Danielle and I enfolded him in an embrace, and then Danielle stepped forward to speak.

"Dad and I would watch the news on TV together and discuss people and their decisions, both good and bad," she said. "I will miss those times on the sofa—giggling sometimes, and other times him sharing wisdom with me about how to move forward in life so as not to harm others or ourselves. He was just so amazing to me and my brother." Danielle's voice began to crack. "I am so sad for us but also for my mom." My baby girl looked over at me. "My mother is now alone, and she and Dad were best friends. We all knew that. For me . . . well, I know what a good husband and father my dad was. I have to believe that Jesus will bring me someone as wonderful. I really do."

I could have done a Holy Ghost dance right there. My spirit was on fire. Mannard had done his job! His life had empowered me and now his children to go after God's best for our lives. Mannard had been a calm spirit, not wild, but he was wildly in love with his family, and because he followed Christ, his love for us and the Lord was apparent for all to see.

. . .

About three years after Mannard's home-going service, the Divas and I stood talking in the church parking lot. We were all too busy to go to a sit-down lunch, but none of us were ready for the conversation to end.

"You better believe we're going on a safari," Brenda said as we discussed our dream trip to Africa. "And I like the idea of doing the safari after the climb."

"Me too," I agreed. Our skirts whipped around in the chilly October wind as we stood by Ang's car. "I don't want to expend any energy that I can use for the mountain. Let's do it after Kilimanjaro. But not overnight in tents with the animals roaming." I gave Ang a pointed look.

"It was just a suggestion," she said. "It would be so cool, though, to hear the animals roam at night."

"Or be their dinner," I added.

Brenda backed me up. "Yes, I just can't do that," she said. "What I'd like to do after the safari—after our long, hard climb—is to just go back to the lodge, you know? To the comforts of beds and sheets!"

"No sleeping outside with the hungry animals, Ang!" I said, cutting to the chase, and we all laughed.

. . .

Three years later, we climbed aboard Nato's Range Rover for the adventure of a lifetime. On day one, we ambled along, taking in the scenery until we came upon a gang of about fifty baboons. Groups of them dangled from trees over a watering hole. Another baboon lounged by itself, using a tree limb like a chaise lounge. The real action started when a midsized baboon made a play for another one's food. He angled over its shoulder and slyly swiped the banana right from the creature's fingers mid-bite!

"Do you see that guy?" Mia said as we watched the offended baboon angrily catch the thief and get him into a headlock. "Does he have a death wish or something?"

Angenette doubled over in laughter. "Shouldn't have taken the 'boon's 'nana! Now he's getting his tail beat."

"Dang, like there's not plenty more," Brenda said. "There's a whole bunch right there." To the right we spotted a large bunch of bananas ripe for the picking.

Ang wiped a tear from her cheek. "He didn't want *those* bananas, he wanted the one in the guy's mouth!"

"He just made it look so appetizing," Brenda said, chuckling.

I laughed too. "Dude just wanted to start trouble."

"Must get boring lying around lazy all day, being polite and all," Ang said. "I guess he just wanted some action, a little drama."

"Well, he's getting it," Brenda said, fixing her camera on the baboon felon, which now stood alone to the side after being pushed out of the group. He turned his back to us and then peered over his shoulder, looking guilty for being caught in the act.

I sat back, enjoying the comedy of the moment. I was thankful everything seemed to be going smoothly. I knew that you can never be sure of your safety when dealing with wild animals in their natural habitat. During my round-the-world cruise, I'd taken a safari, and a lion protecting its young had nearly attacked a fellow passenger. We all had to dive for the floor of the Jeep for protection. None of us had seen the threat coming, and it was a reminder that we never know when a life-altering tragedy may occur. I was no stranger to the truth that life could change in an instant.

We continued on, with Nato searching for wildlife that was photograph worthy. He careened around two other Rovers. Each tour guide was jockeying for the best place to park the vehicles so their passengers could get the ideal photo. We saw a family of vervets and a mother nursing her baby, which looked fresh out of the womb. We saw monkeys, baboons, and a few wild dogs, but none of the big five—rhino, lion, buffalo, leopard, or elephant. Some of the other passengers seemed to be getting antsy.

"I have enough primates on my camera to fill a whole album," Mia said as she used binoculars to scan the terrain.

Nato laughed. "It's so tricky to find the big animals sometimes," he said. "They never stay in one place, yes? They are all over." He kept his eyes on the road, his hands tightly gripping the steering wheel. "I feel bad, you know, when people who travel from so far away don't see what they wish. We want them to get the good ride. My son, Ronnie, he prays for me each morning. He says, 'Poppy, I wish God rains animals on your tour.' He knows how important it is to me that I do well."

"You are doing great!" Ang said. "It's not your fault that the animals need a break from us and our silly cameras."

"We'll see 'em," Mia said with a wink. "They can't hide forever."

Brenda laughed. "We have three full days," she said, leaning her head back into her hands in an exaggerated posture of relaxation. "I'm just enjoying the ride."

We all cracked up.

As I watched the positivity exuding from my friends, I thought about how amazing these women were. Their joy was contagious. They were kind and gracious. They seemed to spread light wherever they went. Christ had brought us together in serving side by side at Christian Tabernacle, but our friendship had become so much more than that. We now believed that God would broaden our territory by bringing us even greater opportunities to spread his light.

Going on a safari together was about so much more than getting the right photo of a lion or an elephant. This journey was about allowing God to deepen our sisterhood as he showed us new things about himself and each other. We bore witness to the beauty of one another's lives as we took in the beauty of God's creation around us.

During the past five years, God had given us a platform. As we chronicled our dares and lived out our friendship publicly on social media, people were watching us. We cared about the example we were setting. We never wanted to become puffed up or boastful about the unique opportunities that had been provided us. We wanted our love for Christ and our sisterhood to be a testimony to the beauty of friendship—how women can support one another in love and help each other to grow.

Back home I had expressed my concern to the Divas that others may view us as flaunting our good fortune. Ang had responded, "We have no control over that. We're not gloating or bragging; we're just sharing a trip. And we make it clear that God is our main focus."

I was thinking about this as we took a lunch break during the safari. Mia and Brenda headed to the ladies' room as Ang and I sat on the edge of a stone, eating the packaged lunch provided by the safari crew. I tore a piece of bread off the loaf and wrapped it around a piece of chicken and cucumber to make a sandwich. "It would just be sad if people see dollar signs and think they can't do what we do. Because let's face it, some folks just can't journey to Africa. They may never have the finances to take a big international trip. In my heart, I want people to see what Christ can do by taking the four of us—little girls who grew up with very little and forged this amazing sisterhood—and equipping us to do all these wonderful things."

Ang nodded. "I hear you, girl. We have to continue to pray that folks hear the real message and that our journeys give them the courage to go outside their comfort zones, no matter what that looks like in their individual lives."

As we were finishing our lunch, Nato raised his walkie-talkie to his ear. "Yes, on our way." He turned to us and shouted, "Ladies, let's board. Got word of a lion around the bend up there."

"Thank goodness!" Brenda said.

"One more baboon and I'd go loony," Mia replied, chuckling under her breath.

We hurried to our ride and climbed aboard as fast as our sore muscles would allow. Nato sped to the spot where two other vehicles were stopped.

A muscular lion lay in front of a basin of water that likely served as the main source of drinking water for the animals. Nothing but dry land surrounded us. As the lion lay there without a care, zebras watched warily and waited along the perimeter.

"Looks like they're waiting for Mr. Big Boy to move," Brenda said.

Nato nodded. "They may be waiting a long time. He doesn't seem eager to leave."

The zebras paced. The lion stood, prowled a few feet, and looked their direction, marking his territory. The zebras edged back and away from the creature that could devour them.

"If you're so thirsty, go find water somewhere else, guys," I said. "You gonna let that dude make you die of thirst?"

"The next water source is not very close," Nato explained. "They are probably thinking they can just wait it out until he tires and moves on to find dinner."

"Or they can *be* dinner," Ang said.

"He likely already feasted and is not hungry," Nato said.

"Yeah, but how can they know that? I wouldn't trust it," Brenda said.

He shrugged and fired up the engine.

"Wait," Brenda said. "Just a minute? The lion has to be ready to go soon. Let's wait and see what happens."

We waited, and after a few minutes the lion stood, stretched, and strutted yards away from the watering hole, creating some distance between himself and the zebras, which slowly made their way to the basin for a drink.

I was surprised by the close proximity of the predator and the prey. Each creature seemed to know its place, and I was amazed once again at God's creation—and his unrivaled power and majesty.

•  •  •

Our Range Rover sped just behind the vehicle ahead. It was the second day of our safari, and we were hot on the trail of one of the big five.

"Hippos!" Nato said, lowering his walkie-talkie. "One of the other drivers saw them." He punched the accelerator, and we all bumped around, hanging on and readying our cameras for whatever we would see.

"I see one!" I pointed to the right of us to where a tusk peeked out from behind some trees. Nato drove closer, and we spotted a great hippopotamus lumbering toward a watering hole. I spotted three other hippos beneath the murky gray water.

"I can't believe we're in Africa!" Mia squealed. "On a safari! Look at us in the motherland, seeing all these creatures out and free."

"What a ride!" Brenda exclaimed, aiming her camera at the scene before us.

As we gazed at the hippos in the pool, we could just barely see the tips of their nostrils. Then another hippopotamus walked right in front of us on his way to join the others.

"He is so big and graceful," Mia said, sitting on the edge of her seat.

I dropped down on my knees to capture a picture through the window. "He sure is walking *slow*. Guess he's got a lot of weight to pull, and what's the rush?"

The hippo pushed his way into the football-shaped pool and lifted each hoof slowly, looking for the perfect spot to rest. Just his presence—watching him do what was normal in his own habitat—thrilled us.

As I watched that beautiful animal settle down to rest in the pool, I thought about my own life. Unlike this hippo, I didn't feel satisfied simply going through my normal routine—working my job, going to the gym, spending time with my kids. But I found myself desiring more. I craved a life that went beyond exciting experiences. I wanted to live from a place of excitement and deep confidence that all things are possible with God.

After I'd taken dozens of resting-hippo photographs, I sat back. The engine hummed as we took in the tranquil scene of birds and hippos splashing and spraying in the water hole. Those beautiful beasts likely knew we were there, but they didn't panic or move from their respite. They were content in their own personal haven.

Sitting in a vehicle watching African wildlife was a welcome reprieve after climbing Kilimanjaro. My body still ached from our trek up and down the mountain.

The Divas and I had decided to do the safari because, as Mia put it, "You don't come all the way to Africa without getting out there and seeing Africa!"

To me, the idea of coming to Africa and not seeing it is like having a life and not living it. What are three things you *need* to do before you leave this planet? How do you plan to accomplish your goals?

• • •

As we drove back to the lodge after our last day in the bush, we stopped at the top of an overpass. In front of us was a guardrail and a stone sign that read "Mount Nero." We surveyed the scene below. It looked as if someone had dropped an atomic bomb, leaving a crater as big as Denver.

"The Ngorongoro Crater," Nato said. "Happened eight thousand years ago. At one time, this now-dormant volcano

was as tall as Mount Kilimanjaro. It's something to see."
Nato talked about the awe-inspiring landscape like it was
his first time seeing it. "It is the centerpiece of Tarangire
National Park. It has fertile land and all sorts of species."

Just beyond the rim of the crater stood lush vegetation
and lakes—the home to thousands of African animals. In
the midst of destruction, life had burst forth. And in its own
way, the crater was beautiful too.

As I viewed its grandeur, I thought of the feat of creating
something out of nothing, then reshaping it into something
altogether new. I wondered why God would use such a harsh
process. But as I have sought the Lord's heart for me in the
midst of my own catastrophic circumstances, I know he allows pain because of his love. While there are some things
I will never understand or know—because he is privy to
information I don't have—I can trust that any change he
institutes is for my benefit and the benefit of his people.

There have been times when I have struggled with God
being all-knowing. I have wanted to hide because of my
sin, which left me feeling ashamed. I could not understand
how he could love me, a person whose nature was not
pure. When tragedy hit, when Mannard died, instead of
immediately turning to my heavenly Father, I turned to prescription drugs. When the pills ran out, instead of turning
to Christ, I turned to alcohol. I tried things to soothe the
pain, to calm the dread of *feeling* that God hadn't come
to my rescue.

But feeling, I would later learn, is not *knowing*. God
knows me—my frailties, my weaknesses, my sin—and he
loves me anyway. And he invites me to know him. He uses
every circumstance—the wonderful and the painful—to

coach, teach, strengthen, correct, and love me into something new, a better version of myself.

I still remember the sickening sense of fear that surged through my body when Mannard died. Why is it human nature to go to fear before faith? As a Christian, I know faith should be my first reaction, yet fear so easily becomes my go-to.

Fear crops up when I experience circumstances over which I have no control: financial calamity, health issues, even worries over the well-being of my adult children as they forge their way in the world. Each day I must choose to ignite the spirit of love from Christ, recognizing that he does not give the spirit of fear "but of power, and of love, and of a sound mind" (2 Tim. 1:7 KJV). That's a truth I need to apply each day.

When I experienced those days of extreme fear following my husband's death, what was so powerful was how the Divas wrapped their arms around me. They cried with me. They held my hand. They handled tasks I had no strength to deal with. And with dare after dare, these faithful friends had never stopped holding me and helping me experience God's love in new ways.

Now, as we traveled through the expanse of the Lake Manyara National Park, I felt deep gratefulness for these women God had put in my life. I thought back to the start of our adventure. When I first saw the park, the largest one in Tanzania and East Africa, my breath caught at the sheer magnitude of it. What I gazed upon was just a portion of what we would travel on our safari.

The metamorphosis of Lake Manyara National Park, where a volcanic eruption resulted in the formation of a crater, is symbolic of the change that can happen to you.

One day you may feel weak and downtrodden, and then later you're strong and optimistic about your future. Are you working on being your strongest? What steps are you taking? You can do it!

• • •

When I think of my life, I think of Africa and that safari. There is a wide chasm between the person I used to be and the person I am now. There is the life I lived with Mannard and the life I lived after Mannard.

When Mannard went to glory, I wanted to stay in that sweet cavern of time where he was breathing and our lives were so richly intertwined. There in that space, I'd watch him grow old. I'd see him fulfill his dreams of world travel, master his motorcycle skills, and learn Spanish. In that alternate reality, I'd see him continue to bless people with the warmth of his heart and touch souls as he shared Christ with them. We'd have grandchildren we would teach and spoil and nourish. He would be such an amazing grandfather and role model.

When he died, my heart broke. The dreams he had—the dreams we had together—broke too. So much of what I longed to see would never happen.

With that man, my life was so good. When he left it, my world went dark. The sunshine he'd brought to each day seemed to be gone. Everywhere I looked, I saw my own failings—a car repossessed, a house in foreclosure, my own weakness in seeking comfort in medication and alcohol. I walked through so many bleak valleys. And yet, through my darkest moments, the Lord had ordered my steps until I found my way back to safe footing.

On the safari, I was aware that even as I roamed God's massive earth, I was not alone. As I had sought God's face during the past six years, his grace had continually shone upon me. He had equipped me to weather everything that had come my way. As we climbed out of the Rover, the wonder of all we had seen still written on our faces, I smiled at my beautiful friends. Brenda placed an arm around my shoulders. With these sister-friends by my side, I had done bold, daring feats I never would have imagined I could do. I had hurled myself out of a plane, conquered dangerous rapids, jumped off a cliff, flown through the air, and climbed the tallest mountain in Africa and the tallest free-standing mountain in the world. These women had unlocked my wild side and helped me find new adventures. With my friends and God by my side, I could take on life with confidence and truly dare to live.

# acknowledgments

When the Lord placed it on my heart to write this book, I was perplexed. "Who, me?" I asked in wonderment. I received a resounding, "YES!" God equipped me with the clarity and recall of all the ways he has been with me throughout life, specifically this journey of loss, healing, and deepening our relationship. God was so gracious to also bring into my life others who offered love, kindness, and whip-sharp talent to guide me through. I give honor, praise, and abundant thanks to Christ for shepherding me.

My agent, Cassie Hanjian, was a critical component in galvanizing the methods and resources and guiding me through my first book effort. I thank you for knowing when to be patient and when to be mightily firm.

Suzanne Gosselin aided me greatly in the initial editorial process as she championed me to dig deeper as we spent months on getting it just right. I simply can't thank you enough.

Nicci Jordan Hubert, Rebekah Guzman, and the entire team at Baker Books were instrumental in helping me power through with insight and spectacular gut instincts. Thank you.

The Dare Divas . . . what can I say? Angenette Frink, Brenda Jegede, and Mia Lewis are three of the smartest, strongest, most beautiful women I know. In service, we grew closer in Christ. In loss, we were resilient and lifted each other up. In adventure, we skydived, whitewater rafted, and climbed Mount Kilimanjaro—together. Christ anointed our friendship, and I thank each of you for being uniquely, lovingly you.

My husband, Michael Sherman—you are my closest confidant, my dearest friend, and my true love. I thank God that he brought a widow and a widower together to share the second half of their lives. I'm also grateful that you allow me to share your beautiful children, Alisa (Eugene) and Angela, and grandchildren Ava and Jonah. I am so blessed.

My mother, Bernice Lyons—I thank you for being my fiercest cheerleader and greatest friend. I got my work ethic from you, Mom. You demonstrated the characteristics of a hardworking woman who wasn't too proud to do work she didn't want to do. I love you dearly.

My children, David and Danielle—I pray that God watches over each of you as you develop your own lives and create your own amazing stories with Christ at the helm. Your dad would be so proud of you, and I am so thankful I get to be your mom. Keep shining. Mom loves YOU!

My grandmother, Callie Hall, and my great-aunt Artherine Harris—I will be forever indebted to you both for being the amazing matriarchs of our family. Grandma, thank you for helping to raise me. I miss you both dearly.

My mom-in-love, Joyce Hasket—you gave me not one but two husbands. You raised an intelligent, warmhearted,

Christ-loving son who meant the world to me and our children. He was the best, and I will forever miss him! When you introduced me to Mike, I resisted, but you insisted. Thank God you did! Mike is just as wonderful as you promised. You are loved, and you will always have a daughter.

Percy, my dad-in-love—how wonderful that we had a strong male in our lives when Mannard went to be with the Lord. You are the best!

Grandmother Covington—your beloved grandson Mannard adored you, and I do too. When I grow up, I want to be just like you.

I thank my pastor, Rev. Dr. James L. Morman, and his wife, Loretta, for being instrumental in my Christian instruction and walk through the good, low, and supernatural times.

I also want to thank Adlai Asante, Paul and Linda Salmon, and Edwin Waites for their dearest friendship over the decades.

Mannard, Mannard, Mannard—you have been the epicenter of my life since I was ten years old. I was mesmerized and fell deeply in love with you. Because you were the head of our family, you left a strong foundation of intellect, wisdom, service, and faith in Christ. We thrive and carry on in your name. We are your legacy!

There are so many others who prayed with me, prayed for me, and offered a smile of encouragement. I thank each of you with all my heart.

God bless!

**Sheri Hunter** served as a media producer for Detroit's national news affiliates, including CBS and NBC, for seven years before transitioning to the print world. She has been a freelance writer for *More* and *National Geographic* magazines. Her story about resilience and sisterhood with her friends the Dare Divas was featured in *Vanity Fair*, *Essence*, *HuffPost*, and *The Hollywood Reporter*. With the Dare Divas she has skydived, whitewater rafted, and most recently climbed Mount Kilimanjaro.

Sheri lives in Michigan with her husband. You can connect with her at sherihunter.com.

# Connect with Sheri

## SheriHunter.com

---

 SheriHunter     AuthorSheriHunter     SheriHunterOfficial